PRAISE FOR *ACE IT!*

"Over the past ten years, Bernie and his team have connected countless sponsors with our show, many of which have become long-term partners. His magic is truly understanding what our partners need while believing in our unique way of delivering. If you want to understand exactly what it takes to become the next sales superstar, this book is for you."

—Elvis Duran, host of "Elvis Duran and the Morning Show"

"The strategies and tactics Bernie Weiss teaches in *Ace It!* work. If you want your sales team to improve its new business results quickly, buy this book for every salesperson in your organization."

—Jennifer Mormile, chief business officer, Condé Nast

"In 25 years of managing sales teams, Bernie is the greatest developer of new business I have seen. His systematic, organized and pragmatic approach can work for anyone willing to put in the time and learn it."

—Stephen Kritzman, senior vice president of sales, Pandora Media

"This really is the only new business sales guide you'll ever need—not only easy to understand, but even easier to implement. Any salesperson who wants to develop new business must read this book."

—Daniel Gallivan, executive director of partnership sales, New York Yankees

"If you want to take control of your sales career, don't just read this book. Study it, and use it. No one can coach you on new business development better than Bernie Weiss."

—Shetellia Riley Irving, vice president of ad sales, Black Entertainment Television (BET)

"Whether you are new to sales or a sales veteran who needs a shot in the arm, follow the sales strategies and tactics presented in this book. Bernie shows a clear path and process to new business success."

—Bob McCuin, EVP/chief revenue officer, Clear Channel Outdoor

ACE IT!

ACE IT!

How Sales Champions Win New Business

BERNIE WEISS

Matt Holt Books
An Imprint of BenBella Books, Inc.
Dallas, TX

BenBella Books, Inc.
10440 N. Central Expressway
Suite 800
Dallas, TX 75231
benbellabooks.com
Send feedback to feedback@benbellabooks.com

BenBella is a federally registered trademark.
Matt Holt and logo are trademarks of BenBella Books.

Printed in the United States of America
10 9 8 7 6 5 4 3 2 1

Library of Congress Location Number: 2021005932
ISBN 9781953295538 (print)
ISBN 9781953295873 (ebook)

Copyediting by James Fraleigh   Text design and composition
Proofreading by Jenny Bridges   by Katie Hollister
  and Sarah Vostok   Cover design by Ty Nowicki
Indexing by Amy Murphy   Printed by Lake Book Manufacturing

Special discounts for bulk sales are available.
Please contact bulkorders@benbellabooks.com.

To my mother, who wrote her book. My father, who never got to write his. And my wife, who will write hers one day.

CONTENTS

DISCOVER

TEACH

CLARIFY

PRESENT

ASK

LAUNCH

FOREWORD

The best companies, the best sales teams, and the best salespeople don't just have one good new business month; they are able to sustain new business growth quarter after quarter and year after year. And even though technology has changed many aspects of how we sell, with more technological disruption always on the way, there will continue to be many lucrative career opportunities for salespeople willing to take responsibility for identifying and creating their own sales opportunities—to connect the dots to develop new business. To do that, you need a systematic sales approach that is both effective and efficient. You need to stand out from the competition by positioning yourself as a true business partner who consistently creates value for your clients.

If you have been wondering how top performers produce greater new business results than their peers, this book provides the answers. Over the last ten years at iHeartMedia, I have seen firsthand that the new business sales approach Bernie Weiss is teaching works. In *Ace It!*, Bernie doesn't just cover sales theory; he provides a strategic roadmap for new business success, including detailed frameworks, scripts, and real-world tips that you can immediately apply in your day-to-day sales efforts.

If you are seeking a competitive advantage that will set you apart from your colleagues and competition, in *Ace It!* Bernie gives you the master plan.

—Bob Pittman
Chairman and CEO
iHeartMedia, Inc.

PROLOGUE

I t is a cold late afternoon in March and I am walking down Manhattan's "Piano Row" near Carnegie Hall. Piano Row was once famous for being the home to close to a dozen piano stores. Unfortunately, many have since closed.

A couple of months before, I'd bought a house, and I am struggling with what to do with an empty room adjacent to the living room. Someone suggested a piano would look good there, and although I haven't played since I was twelve, the idea of having a grand piano in my house that I can start playing again is appealing. So, for the first time in my life, I am in the market for a piano.

This afternoon, my plan is to stop in at two piano showrooms on Piano Row. The first one is called Faust Harrison Pianos.

The moment I enter, a well-dressed salesperson in his early thirties named Tom approaches me. Friendly, firm handshake, good eye contact, eager to help and get started, he says, "Let me show you around. We have many great pianos in our showroom right now. I am sure you'll find one you like."

He walks me to the first piano, a beautiful Yamaha, and I immediately realize that Tom really knows what he is talking about. He explains the name of the model, exact measurements, year it was built, where it was built, its price point, financing options, and its availability in black, brown, and even white. I am impressed. He even hands me a beautifully produced glossy Yamaha brochure before we continue to the next grand piano, a Steinway. Based on all the facts Tom is rattling off, it seems to be the better piano, and of course it is also an American heritage brand. I am intrigued, but the price is higher than what I am planning to spend.

"Don't worry. We are just getting started. You don't have to be anywhere, do you?" Tom asks, as he shows me a new Bösendorfer piano, famous for its intricate Austrian handcraftsmanship. As Tom is running through the specs, I am flipping through another glossy brochure, trying to figure out what's different compared to the pianos I already saw.

On we go: a Bechstein, another Yamaha—this time a used one—a Hoffmann, and several more.

"Oh wow, it's already after six. I really need to run," I say eventually. "Thanks so much for all the information and for being so helpful."

"No problem at all. That's what I am here for. Here is one more brochure about our store and here is my business card. Of course, you can always call me if you have a specific question on any of the pianos—24–7!"

I put the brochures into my briefcase and walk a couple of buildings east to take a quick look at what the second store I had heard about, Allegro Pianos, has to offer. Since this store is closing at 6:30 PM and I don't see any customers inside, I almost feel like an intruder. They are probably trying to close up shop for today.

"Anything I can help with?" someone yells from across the room. Since some of the lights in the store are already turned off, I have a hard time seeing him.

"Yes, I wanted to take a quick look at the pianos you have in store. I am sorry I got here so late."

"Well, why don't you come in," he says after a short pause, not making me feel particularly welcome. As he is walking across the showroom to greet me, I have enough time to size him up. With a rumpled suit, unkempt hair, and a bit overweight, he reminds me of an old college professor of mine.

"I am Ori Bukai, the store owner. Nice to meet you. Why don't we go to my office and have a little chat."

We sit down on two very comfortable sofas in his spacious office in the back of his store and Ori pours me a drink.

"When I opened this store fifteen years ago, I wanted to be known for two things: a great liquor cabinet, with a ton of choices, and a selection of pianos that is a little bit off the mainstream. Smaller brands, many crafted by hand, which have a distinct sound and are also beautiful to look at. The type of piano you will get compliments on when you have guests over at your house. I guess if we would be in the car industry, we would be Alfa Romeo. But now tell me, why are you looking for a piano?"

I tell him about the new house and my idea of picking up playing again.

"Buying a piano is a big decision. Just think about what else you can buy for the money. A car, a nice painting, or a country club membership, for example. Owning a piano, though, is life changing. It is something you will have forever, for the rest of your life, and then pass on to the next generation. My grandmother's piano is one of my most prized possessions. You'll also find learning and playing really rewarding and will impress everyone from your mother-in-law to your dinner party guests. Tell me, when was the last time you played?"

"About thirty years ago. I took classes for about six years as a kid, but stopped when I was thirteen. I mostly played classical music back then. Beethoven, Chopin, Mozart. I could never figure out how to play contemporary music. Billy Joel, Elton John, Queen."

"It's much easier to learn these things now. You just need to go to YouTube and follow along. So your goal is to play more modern music? Pop music?"

"I think so, yes. That's really the type of music I usually listen to."

"Great! Tell me more about the room the piano will be in. How big is it? Does it have a window? What else is in it?"

"About three hundred square feet I guess, with one window. There is really not much else in it, other than a bookshelf that fully covers one wall."

I am starting to wonder why this is important, but Ori explains.

"It's important for me to visualize the room. Plays a big role when it comes to sound."

I describe it in more detail and even end up drawing a floor plan of the room, indicating where I think the piano should stand.

"Ah, you would be able to look out into your garden if you position it like that. Excellent."

Ori's questions continue for about twenty minutes.

"Where is the house located?"

"Who will you be playing for? Who will be listening when you practice?"

"How much do you want to invest?"

"Which piano brands do you know? Any particular ones you are more interested in than others?"

"Are you planning to play for guests as well? Entertain them with your music?"

"When will you be playing the most? In the morning? On the weekend?"

Suddenly, Ori jumps up and excitedly asks me to follow him into the showroom.

"I think I have the right grand piano for you."

He walks me back into the showroom, to a beautiful black Estonia piano. He sits down and starts to play. First, Elton John's "Mona Lisas and Mad Hatters," followed by Queen's "Bohemian Rhapsody." The music sounds wonderful.

"Estonia only produces one hundred pianos a year. It's a very exclusive brand," Ori says, then goes on to explain the characteristics of this particular model and why he thinks it is perfect for someone like me.

"Why don't you sit down and try it?"

You don't have to guess at which store I end up purchasing my piano. While I didn't fully commit during my first visit, I never went to another store and never looked at another piano than the one Ori chose for me. The piano costs about 30 percent more than what I had originally budgeted, but I am justifying it by telling myself that it's a good investment—and that I will sound so much better on this Estonia.

Four weeks later, the piano is delivered, and I put it exactly where Ori and I had planned it in his office.

GAME, SET, AND MATCH

I f you followed men's tennis in the 1980s, you know that the most dominant players at the time were American John McEnroe and Czechoslovakian Ivan Lendl. In the history of tennis, there has probably never been a more natural tennis talent than John McEnroe. He had a unique style that couldn't be taught or copied, and he possessed a special talent: a distinct feel for the ball on the racket, especially at the net. With his aggressive serve-volley approach, he was able to impose his type of play on his opponents. He "read" his opponents' shots accurately before they even hit the ball and instinctively moved to the right positions on the court. A lot of McEnroe's game had to do with instinct, and he constantly invented new shots and new angles. He was a talent that comes around only once in a generation. You can think of John McEnroe as a Natural-Born Tennis Player.

But would it have been a good idea for junior players (like me) to model their games after McEnroe? No, because it would have been almost impossible. That's why most players back then tried to follow closer in the footsteps of Ivan Lendl, one of the first offensive baseline players in men's tennis, and someone who had a much bigger impact on the next generation of tennis players than McEnroe. Just think of Jim Courier, Andre Agassi, and Thomas Muster. They all had a strong forehand, excellent footwork, good mental game, and the ability to play for five hours without letting up, after putting themselves through grueling conditioning workouts to prepare for a tournament.

But most importantly, Lendl approached his game very systematically. Many of his points were constructed the same way. He returned the ball to the center of the court, very deep to the baseline. He moved toward the backhand side of the baseline to open up the court with an inside-out forehand. He stepped up to start dominating the rally with his forehand, first to the left corner, then to the right. Once he had his opponent on the run, he had his choice of shots to finish the point, usually a crushing top-spin forehand.

Thousands of hours of training went into being able to pull off points like this. And Lendl needed them, because he created and followed a system. He broke down a point into several mini-steps, all of which had to be completed for Lendl to maximize his chance of winning it. You can think of Ivan Lendl as a Systematic Tennis Player, the exact opposite of a Natural-Born Tennis Player like John McEnroe. Because of their totally different approaches to the sport, their duels were entertaining to watch.

Who was more successful? Ivan Lendl won eight Grand Slam trophies, John McEnroe seven. But that's not the point. The point is that 99 percent of salespeople will be more successful by following Lendl's process-driven approach than McEnroe's improvisational style.

DIFFERENT, BUT THE SAME

While every sale is different, every sale is really the same. Each sale is unique because sales champions not only find a way for each of their customers to feel special but also to tailor their products and services closely to the clients' needs. They make adjustments based on the type of business, the personality of the person to whom they are selling, and even the physical setting of the sales pitch. But almost all sales also follow the same pattern. That's why every sale is also identical. The salespeople who are effective during every step of the sales process, from prospecting to asking for the order and implementing the solution they sold, are the ones who are consistently beating their new business budgets.

Having a framework that you follow every single time you attempt a sale can turn you into a sales superstar. Sales champions excel when they figure out how to win new business and then replicate their approach over and over. And if you follow the process and concentrate on each individual step of it, deals will happen automatically, without using any fancy closing techniques. The more you can break down the sales process into individual steps, the quicker you can become a true expert in each of them. No wonder Ivan Lendl became a much more successful tennis coach than John McEnroe in their second careers. Lendl had a systematic process, broken down to the last detail, that he could pass on, while McEnroe did not.

SALES CAN BE TAUGHT

Sales is a science that can be taught. I'm the best example of this fact. Not once until my twenty-seventh birthday had I ever considered sales as a career. In college, I majored in marketing and finance. My internships were in the banking industry, and certainly not sales related. My first job was as a management consultant, almost as far from sales as possible. But in the 1990s, when—partly by coincidence—I landed a job in the media industry, it became clear to me that to have a successful career there, I would quickly have to learn how to sell advertising.

To maximize my sales success, I wanted to develop a sales system that I could follow every day. I started by reading as much literature on sales as I could find, attending sales trainings and conferences, listening to sales tapes (yes, cassettes back then), and also meeting with some of the best account managers and sales managers across different industries, trying to pick their brains. Most importantly, though, I was able to put what I learned into practice day after day: trying out new things, doing more of the tactics that worked and fewer of the ones that didn't. For several years I studied the sales game, until I was confident that my system could be applied successfully in one of the toughest sales markets and industries on the planet: New York's media industry, where thousands of salespeople on hundreds of different sales teams compete for billions of advertising dollars.

As I followed my sales system, my results came quicker than I expected. Eight months after joining iHeartMedia (back then still called Clear Channel Radio), America's number-one audio company operating

850 radio stations in more than 150 markets across America, I was ranked first in annual new business sales among all one hundred account executives of its New York sales team. In my last year as an account executive, I was ranked in the top new business tier of all 1,700 iHeartMedia salespeople countrywide, which ultimately led to my promotion to sales management and, many years later, to president of iHeartMedia's New York City broadcast operation, where I oversee some of the most prestigious radio brands in the world.

It never would have happened if I hadn't followed my systematic sales approach, which over the past fifteen years I have taught to hundreds of iHeartMedia employees. Many of these account executives went on to become sales superstars and rose to leadership positions themselves. Our group became New York's top-ranked radio enterprise by revenue. This book outlines the successful sales system that I battle-tested and many other sales professionals have proven.

OVERVIEW

There are many, many sales books available. I know because over my twenty-year sales career, working around the world, I've read a ton of them. But the books rarely offer advice that works in the real world. To succeed as a salesperson, you need answers to questions like:

- "I was so close to making the sale, but now my prospect is 'ghosting' me. How do I get them to engage with me again?"
- "How do I identify myself on a cold call?"
- "What do I say to a prospect at the start of our first meeting?"
- "Should I leave voicemails or not?"
- "How do I respond to objections on a cold call or during a proposal presentation?"
- "At what point in a meeting do I talk about my company and our capabilities?"
- "How do I grab the attention of someone when I reach out by email or on LinkedIn for the first time?"

- "How do I get my prospect to agree to do business with me?"
- "What's the best technique for arriving at a clear assignment and budget?"
- "I found a great lead, but the person doesn't pick up the phone and doesn't respond to emails. Anything else I can do to get in the door?"
- "How do I negotiate the best sales outcome for the company I represent?"

It's the basics that trip people up. That's why following a systematic sales process in a disciplined way is the best way to sustained sales success.

The book is divided into ten sections, each representing one step of the sales process as shown in the "Ten-Step Sales Framework" figure. Two of these—"Commit" and "Ask"—are so important in sales that they apply and extend across all phases of the process.

The first section, "Commit," explores the importance of having the right attitude and level of preparedness throughout the sales process. Being strong in this area has a massive influence on sales success—potentially

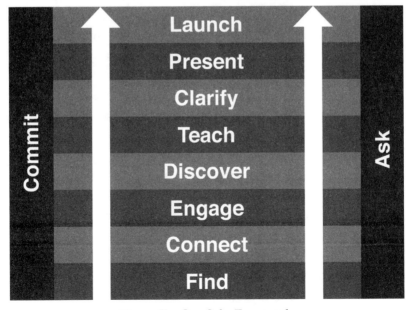

Figure: Ten-Step Sales Framework

even the greatest. Salespeople who might not be as technically savvy as others can still outperform by being mentally tough as well as disciplined.

The second section, "Find," focuses on creating lead profiles you will use to identify and evaluate new business prospects. We will explore the best ways to look for leads and how an efficient prospecting system can help you be more productive.

The third section, "Connect," covers all strategies and tactics you will use to set up face-to-face meetings with prospects. We will introduce scripts and templates for cold calls, seed emails, and LinkedIn messages, then address how successful salespeople deal with objections.

The fourth section, "Engage," explores the first face-to-face meeting with the prospect, in person or on video. It describes how to stay in control of the meeting and introduces an easy-to-follow meeting framework that helps keep your meetings on track.

The fifth section, "Discover," gives examples for effective listening techniques and insightful questions that help you uncover challenges a prospect might have.

The sixth section, "Teach," covers how sales champions impress prospects with insights and new perspectives, and reviews what type of information they bring to the first meeting.

The seventh section, "Clarify," gives tips on how to arrive at a mutually agreed-upon budget and how to leave your first prospect meeting with a clearly defined assignment.

The eighth section, "Present," focuses on the importance of creating customer-centric proposals. It provides a checklist of tactics that will make your sales presentations more effective.

The ninth section, "Ask," shows how asking for mini-commitments throughout the sales process is more successful than any artificial closing technique. It also discusses the negotiation tactics sales aces use to maximize their order sizes.

The tenth and last section, "Launch," describes how exemplary implementation and execution work ensures renewals and long-term client relationships.

To show how these sales strategies work, you will meet a fictional prospect called "Rebecca Gyms." This will make the scripts, responses, sales material, negotiation techniques, and other tactics more realistic, and will allow you to immediately apply the content to your day-to-day sales work.

THIS BOOK IS FOR YOU

This book was written with a few different audiences in mind:

- People who have recently switched careers
- Recent college graduates who want to pursue a sales job
- Sales veterans who have plateaued and need a boost to jump-start their careers
- Sales managers who are looking for a sales process that will help train their new hires to produce significant revenue quickly

If your day-to-day responsibilities include finding new leads and turning them into revenue generators, this is the book for you! While many of the examples and scripts are taken from the media industry, where an advertising sales executive typically sells to a business owner, marketing manager, or the C-suite, these concepts are also applicable to retail industries selling products and services that have higher price points, like cars—or pianos.

COMMIT

1

ARE YOU ALL IN?

Sales is a science that can be taught to almost everyone. However, that doesn't mean everyone will be equally successful at it. While the fundamentals can be taught, a winning attitude, a positive mindset, and 100 percent commitment cannot. To be great in sales, you need to be fully committed to your sales career. Several studies have shown that when salespeople fail, more than half of the time the reasons are related to attitude, not technical skills.

I often meet with college graduates who tell me that they want to "try sales as a career." And every single time I tell them to not even bother. Once you have made the choice to pursue a sales career, you have to be all in. Just "trying it" or being 99 percent sure you want to be a salesperson are recipes for disaster.

Successful salespeople are proud to be in sales. When they are asked at a dinner party about their profession, they will not hesitate to proudly and loudly proclaim, "I am in sales." They believe in what they are doing, which is helping others be more successful, and they believe in the company they work for. They are certainly not "embarrassed" to be in sales (yes, I have met and worked with too many talented people who were, and it never ended well). Why wouldn't you be proud of working in sales? Sales is one of the few careers that allows you to be the master of your own destiny. The more hours you work, the more calls you make, the more qualified prospects you meet, the more proposals you write and present, the more deals you will strike and the more money you will make (assuming you are compensated on some kind of commission or bonus plan). It's as simple as that.

FOCUS ON THE WINS

There are not many jobs that reward productivity as much as a sales job. What's not to like?

Most people will answer that question with one word: *REJECTION*. And not just any rejection. Constant, daily, maybe unfair and sometimes cruel rejection. Rejection can—and will—happen during every single step in the sales process. The hang-up on the first phone call, being turned down for a follow-up meeting, the dismissal of your concept or idea, the refusal to entertain more detailed price negotiations. Rejection happens all the time in sales. The question is how you deal with it.

What sales champions understand is that what's being rejected is not themselves. They don't take it personally, understanding that rejection is part of the job. Sales is a series of defeats interrupted by revenue-generating wins. Salespeople who get too hung up on the defeats instead of remaining focused on the wins are the ones who get easily frustrated and potentially even burn out. Salespeople who stay positive throughout are the ones who eventually enjoy more, and better, client relationships. Once the enthusiasm about a closed deal sets in, all the rejection leading up to it is quickly forgotten.

But I certainly don't want to sugarcoat it. Sales is hard. Many people can't deal with the uncertainty of wondering if a deal is closing or not, the fluctuating paychecks, the unexpected cancellations, and other obstacles that appear out of nowhere. However, rejection and uncertainty, taken together, are the main reason why salespeople make more money than most people who have to rely on a modest 2 to 3 percent annual cost of living raise.

KNOW YOUR LIMITS

Not everyone is built to succeed in a sales-hunter role, though. I have worked with many account managers who were excellent negotiators, provided incredible customer service, and were extremely well-liked by their existing clients. In fact, if I as a manager ever attempted to make a change in their clients' coverage, all hell would break loose, with the clients literally fighting for "their" account manager. But, partly because these salespeople were so focused on their existing client relationships, many of them struggled mightily when it came to developing new business, overcoming objections, convincing prospects to change direction, or even setting up meetings with potential new clients in the first place. These valued colleagues ultimately succeeded in a service role, which was more tailored to their strengths. New business developers need to be comfortable with the tension and the pressure that can arise during every single step of the sales process.

DON'T OVERTHINK IT

Have you ever worked with someone who was so analytical and so focused on having 100 percent of the answers that he or she rarely ever took any action? That's another type of personality that has a hard time in new business sales. I am certainly not advocating that you don't go fully prepared into a sales call and not do research leading up to it—far from it. But if analysis turns into paralysis, when the search for data and facts becomes so dominating that it interferes with the day-to-day selling, you will not be able to maximize your sales success.

It's good to think through potential objections before a meeting; sales champions do that. But once you start to mentally agree with these objections, you begin to unconsciously torpedo your best efforts. Despite the best and most proven sales systems, despite all the information readily available on the internet, new business sales can be messy. You will never have all of the information, and you will never be able to fully anticipate what will happen on a sales call. We all have had embarrassing moments while selling. Get used to them, because you certainly can't fully avoid them. In fact, if you do, you are probably not taking enough risks. New business sales is for action-oriented people, and analysis paralysis is not a quality that will lead you to sales success.

ACT LIKE A BUSINESSPERSON, NOT A SALESPERSON

I am actually pretty uncomfortable with the term "sales hunter." I only used it to try to make the point that new business sales requires a very proactive mindset and approach. But would I ever want to position myself to a prospect or client as a sales hunter? Absolutely not. People love to buy, but they hate to be sold. Unfortunately, amateurish sales techniques that have existed over many decades have given the sales profession a bad reputation. Clients want to be educated with insights and new information. They want engaging meetings with someone who understands their challenges and their business. In short, they want to deal with businesspeople rather than salespeople.

In an ideal scenario, your prospects will perceive you to be on the same level as they are. That's not an easy thing to accomplish, especially when you deal with the C-suite or business owners. To make this a reality, you have to establish yourself quickly as an expert in your area.

"But I'm not CEO or general manager of the company I represent. How can you expect me to do that?"

First, you don't have to have a title to earn someone's respect. Secondly, and more importantly, no one is expecting you to be an expert in all areas of your prospect's business. That would be impossible. You need to be an expert in the area where your expertise and the prospect's challenges—and potential solutions—intersect.

Sometimes it's the combination of several seemingly insignificant actions that brand you as a salesperson and not a businessperson. I worked with several salespeople who would start out every first sales call with a prospect with, *"Thank you so much for taking the time; I know how busy you must be"*—not an effective way to start a meeting at all. Why? You just

SALESPEOPLE . . .	BUSINESSPEOPLE . . .
. . . are doing most of the talking	. . . ask the right questions
. . . are mostly talking about their company, its capabilities, and themselves	. . . challenge with insights and new information
. . . are trashing the competition	. . . offer advice and are considered a resource
. . . are only focused on "the close"	. . . are perceived as strategic partners, not vendors
. . . are begging for a "test"	. . . know their time is valuable and will only work on clear, mutually agreed-upon assignments that include a budget figure and KPIs
. . . are talking about price, discounts, and special offers way too early	. . . come up with innovative solutions
. . . care only about hitting their monthly quota and not about the client's business	. . . determine early on how they can measure the results of their offerings at the client level
. . . overpromise and underdeliver	. . . execute and deliver on their promises
. . . use "salesy" language like "exciting opportunity," "one-of-a-kind idea," "amazing offer," or "we are #1, the best, biggest, smartest, cheapest, quickest"	. . . use terms like "profit margin," "return on investment," and "competitive advantage"
. . . think it helps the cause if you mention the prospect's first name as often as possible	. . . show confident body language, including a firm handshake and good eye contact

Figure 1.1: Salespeople vs. Businesspeople

artificially, voluntarily, and unnecessarily lowered your level by making prospects feel they are doing you a favor by meeting with you. Trust me, the last people busy executives want to deal with are overanxious sales-people who are literally begging for business.

Positioning yourself on the same level as your counterpart takes discipline and confidence. Remind yourself of all the reasons that you should be taken seriously before every interaction with a prospect. Maybe it's the company itself. Maybe it's a success story you are responsible for. Maybe it's a new and creative idea.

Conventional wisdom has long held that B2B sales is all about building relationships because relationships are the foundation of sales success. The advice "Build relationships first and sales will follow" has existed for decades in the sales world. However, more recent studies have shown that relationship-centric selling may be less effective than it used to be, as clients increasingly care more about value, insights, and return on investment. Relationships are still important, but a great client relationship may be the result—not the cause—of successful selling.

MENTAL TOUGHNESS

Your mindset in approaching the sale will determine the outcome more than any other element of the sales process. If you are sitting down with a potential new client and think about all the reasons this prospect might have to *not* buy from you, most likely this will harm your sales results. If you wouldn't buy from yourself, why should anyone else? Instead, if you have a winner's attitude, and visualize before you even meet with the prospect how you are making the sale—the way athletes visualize a win or a goal—your chances of making the sale will be much higher.

Henry Ford said, "Whether you think you can or you think you can't, you're right."

And if you don't believe Mr. Ford, heed the words of Michael Jordan, the greatest basketball player of all time: "You have to expect things of yourself before you can do them."

When coaching the iHeartMedia team in New York, one of my goals is to get the salespeople to actively visualize the call *before* they pick up the phone to reach out to a new prospect. What I want them to picture are not just the 850 radio stations they are representing, but the 277 million listeners these stations are reaching each month. They are visualizing the 277 million consumer relationships they are representing and that they are willing to rent out to unaffiliated third parties like the prospect they are calling. With 277 million people, how can you not be self-confident? Thinking about your company, product, or service in that way can raise your confidence level.

One of the most successful salespeople I know has the habit of pumping himself up during the elevator ride up to the prospect's floor. A fist pump combined with a loud "It's go time!" puts him in the right mental state. Once the elevator door opens, he is in his zone.

Will every deal you are pursuing result in a sale because of all your optimism? Of course not. But that doesn't mean you should ever walk into a prospect meeting with anything less than the self-confidence of knowing that the prospect needs you, your company, and your product or service. In addition, your confidence level will be higher the more prepared you are, the more research you have done leading up to the call, the more effective the questions you have devised, and the better the customized solution you are about to present is. Preparation provides self-assurance.

CONSTANTLY RAISING THE BAR

Being *all in* means you are making a conscious commitment to becoming a student of the sales game, a lifelong learner. Sales champions develop an obsession with doing things better. The reality is that if you are not consistently adding to your sales skills, not only are you running the risk of being outsold by your competition; eventually, you will also become obsolete. It is mind-blowing and quite frankly shocking how few hands go up when I ask in sales trainings who is currently reading a book about sales. Thank goodness *you* are clearly not falling into this category, but you get my point. In an age when so much relevant information is at your fingertips—from articles and blogs to YouTube videos and podcasts—it is borderline criminal not to take advantage of it.

All of us can figure out a way to carve out just thirty minutes a day, Monday through Friday, to work on our sales game. That's two and a half hours per week, ten hours per month, and about 125 hours per year, the equivalent of three full workweeks or fifteen workdays. You'll need the discipline to do it for longer than just a few weeks. Maybe it will even cost you twenty-five dollars a month to get access to whatever information you choose. But don't you think you would experience transformative change and raise your sales game to the next level by committing to this? Trust me, it will pay off many times over.

Dr. Bob Rotella, author of *How Champions Think*, tells the story of Paul Runyan, who won the PGA Golf Championship in 1934 and 1938, then devoted his life to teaching golf with the same commitment and excellence he brought to competitive play. He never gave up trying to improve his own game, all the way into his eighties and even early nineties.

One day, Paul was speaking at a convention for teaching professionals. He was, by then, around ninety years old.

"Thank you so much for bringing me back. I'm thrilled to be here again this year," Paul began. "But I have to apologize to you. Last year, I promised you that I was going to practice my short game for at least two hours every day. I am embarrassed to tell you that on three days last year, I did not honor my commitment."

Any questions?

The best part about committing yourself to continuous improvement is that not only will your sales skills improve, your confidence level will progress as well. Remember, attitude and confidence is half the battle in sales. Clients want to deal with the best of the best. And if you want to become part of that elite group, you have to put in the work.

IT'S THE CUSTOMER, STUPID!

A positive attitude, commitment to personal improvement, discipline, visualizing success, grit, and resilience in the wake of objections and uncertainty will take you very far in sales. But they can't take you all the way. To unlock your full sales potential, you need a totally customer-focused mindset. Of course you want to make the sale, and of course you want to earn a big commission, but your primary motivation needs to be that you are doing right by your customer. If your number-one goal in sales is to make your client more successful, you have set yourself up for a long and prosperous sales career.

Think about how liberating this approach is. If you truly believe that you and the company you represent have something to offer that addresses a clear client need, suddenly the dreaded cold call starts to feel more like a favor you are doing for the people you are contacting. If you didn't call them to set up a meeting, wouldn't they miss out on an opportunity that would make a huge difference to their business? Wouldn't they be foolish not to sit down with you? You are not calling to interrupt; you are calling because you can help. Just having this different mindset makes a huge difference. Everything changes when your ultimate goal is to help your potential client.

FIND

2

THE RIGHT PROSPECTING PHILOSOPHY

I love prospecting! I have always found it to be the most motivating aspect of the entire sales process, especially when you dig up a lead that no one else on your team and none of your competitors have been able to uncover. Once you find a great lead, you can't wait to reach out and connect with the prospect.

DIGGING FOR GOLD

Maybe I like digging for leads because it's in my blood. In 1896, my great-great-grandfather left his entire family behind in Austria to travel to the Klondike region in the Pacific Northwest and dig for gold. If you think the "gold digging" analogy is far-fetched, think again. I have never personally searched for gold, but a quick Google search takes you to several "How to Search for Gold" articles that in essence suggest the following:

- A strategic approach is key. It's critical to narrow your search down to areas that have not only produced gold, but where *big* gold nuggets (weighing more than one ounce) have been found. There are countless mining districts across the United States and around the world that have produced many thousands of ounces of gold. However, high gold production doesn't necessarily mean large gold nuggets. In fact, it rarely does. The vast majority of these districts produce fine flakes and dust, but only a limited number of larger nuggets. There are hundreds of miners who recover more than one hundred ounces of gold per year, none of it larger than a pencil eraser.
- Searching for large gold nuggets takes a totally different approach than searching for smaller ones. To have any realistic chance of stumbling across one, you need to move some serious dirt first. You start with a bigger area and then almost surgically narrow it down.
- There is no magic-bullet answer for how to research gold deposits. Talking to locals in a known district, reading old government documents and historic newspaper articles, and any number of other sources may provide you with that one shred of knowledge that will lead you to the next nugget patch. This process can be frustrating, but ultimately to your benefit: this knowledge is not that easy for other miners to gain, which increases your chances of being the first.
- The common methods like gold panning and sluicing will find you gold, but they don't process much material. Newer technologies like metal detectors are specifically designed to "see" large pieces of gold and cover a lot of ground efficiently.
- Don't let anyone tell you all the big gold nuggets have been found. Experts believe 90 percent of the earth's gold remains undiscovered.

Sound familiar? If you have worked in B2B sales, it should. Effective and efficient prospecting, the process of uncovering potential high-value targets, follows very similar principles, which we will cover in the next few pages.

But let's first clarify the term "prospecting." The term has been defined in several ways. Sometimes it refers to cold calling or other efforts to set up a meeting with a prospect. Or it is used as more of an umbrella term that encompasses finding, researching, *and* contacting leads. For our purposes, prospecting explicitly relates to all the activities undertaken to identify and evaluate leads. It does *not* include your attempts to actually contact prospects to set up meetings. That will be covered in the next section, "Connect."

For the following discussion and the rest of this book, we are using the terms "lead" and "prospect" interchangeably, and the term "buyer" when we are referring to the actual person we are dealing with in the process.

THERE ARE MANY BAD LEADS

The number-one reason salespeople are not seeing success is that they are not capable of finding the right prospects to call, and therefore waste valuable time with the wrong prospects. Let that sink in for a moment. The number-one reason salespeople fail is not that they are bad at closing deals or presenting, or that they don't know the product or service they are trying to sell. Failing to close deals is tied to something that happens much earlier in the sales process, during the step that unexperienced salespeople consider the "easy" part of it all—prospecting!

How hard can it be? All you have to do is look around and make a list of companies to call on. The longer the list, the better, correct?

"Every lead is a good lead. You never know where your next sale is coming from."

"You can't have too many leads."

"I am changing up my prospects all the time."

I hear these statements all the time in coaching sessions or during interviews with potential sales candidates. They are just not true.

"Walk me through your prospecting approach" has actually become one of my favorite interview questions for sales recruits. The response tells you a lot about how someone approaches this very important part of the sales chain. Is prospecting seen as a highly strategic activity that needs to be as structured and planned as possible? Or is the person just writing down names of companies by hand in a notebook? Even the most gifted salespeople will not produce good results if they are calling on the wrong accounts.

Strategic prospecting means effective and efficient prospecting. It is about consciously choosing the prospects in which to invest your time—your most precious asset—and which ones to avoid.

Jordan Belfort (the Wolf of Wall Street) tells the story about a cocky young salesman in his brokerage firm, who—in a role-play training situation—is asked to sell a pen to Jordan. The salesperson starts with typical sales talk and runs through features and benefits, lets Jordan try out the pen, even offers a massive discount if he would buy it "right now." Jordan shuts him down quickly. No sale, far from it!

One of the senior guys of his firm comes in and Belfort decides to ask the same thing of him:

"I want you to sell me this pen. Show the kid how it's done."

"Fine, I'll sell it to you."

"So, Jordan, tell me, how long have you been in the market for a pen?"

"I'm not, actually. I never use pens!"

"Really? Well, then you can have your lousy pen back," replies the sales pro, tossing the pen back onto Jordan's desk. Then he looks at the young salesman: "I don't sell things to people who don't need them. I leave that to novices like you!"

During the prospecting phase, it is usually not possible to ascertain with 100 percent certainty if a lead is a perfect fit for what you are offering. But using the right prospecting philosophy, strategy, and tactics will maximize your chances.

EXISTING CLIENTS ARE GREAT PROSPECTS

The best prospects for new business generation are your present customers. While growing existing accounts and upselling new products or services to existing clients are not the primary focus of this book, the closing ratio will be much higher with an existing client than with a prospect with whom you have never done business. How can it not be? You already have an existing personal relationship with the client, which means you can be sure the client will be taking your call. You know the client's challenges, goals, and key performance indicators (KPIs), and hopefully you have established at least some level of mutual trust and confidence. And these clients most likely have established credit terms and have paid you in the past. In fact, many of the new leads effective salespeople are looking for during the prospecting phase are modeled after their existing successful clients.

OF POST-IT NOTES AND IMAGINARY LEAD LISTS

When struggling salespeople seek me out for sales advice, I first ask to see their lead list. Actually, I have been trying to impress upon my teams' sales managers to make consistent review of their sales forces' lead lists their highest priority. You wouldn't believe some of the lead lists I have seen over the years. I don't even necessarily mean the type of leads on the lists. We will get to those. I am talking about the lists themselves. I have seen them as fifteen yellow Post-its, perfectly aligned on a desk next to the keyboard. I have seen them in handwritten notebooks, with words crossed out and written over, on separate pages, some even half ripped out, with names of prospects underlined three times or circled twice. I have seen them on whiteboards, color-coded with fourteen different markers. I have seen them in the form of multi-page printouts from certain databases or directories. And sometimes I did not see them at all, because the salesperson "had them all in my head, no need for me to write them down." In an age of customer relationship management (CRM) systems like Salesforce, this, of course, all seems very arbitrary and even amateurish. We will cover more of this in chapter four, but suffice it to say that none of the aforementioned approaches can be described as strategic, effective, or efficient.

SEGMENTING, LIMITING, AND PRIORITIZING LEAD LISTS

Peter F. Drucker, considered by many to be the father of management thinking, wrote in his classic *The Effective Executive*: "If there is any one 'secret' of effectiveness, it is concentration; effective executives do first things first and they do one thing at a time."

Applied to sales purposes in general and prospecting in particular, "concentration" means that instead of spinning our wheels with the wrong prospects and too many of them, lead lists should be:

- segmented
- limited
- prioritized

Making sure your lead list is **segmented** forces you to become an expert in a certain territory (e.g., Long Island); a certain vertical, industry, or category (e.g., automotive); or a certain type of business (e.g., start-ups). There are many advantages to this approach. It will certainly make your prospecting efforts more focused as you quickly notice certain patterns for each segment (e.g., what type of media automotive dealerships on Long Island usually use to advertise, and what's the best way to monitor that). It will also boost your confidence as you learn more about a specific industry. You become familiar with certain technical terms used (e.g., number of "ups," meaning the number of potential customers coming into a car dealership) and with common challenges that all businesses in a segment are facing (e.g., that auto dealerships' margins on new car sales are deteriorating). Over time, you will build a portfolio of case studies that will help you get more assignments. You will also better understand what type of solutions work best for customers in a specific segment. In short, it will be much easier for you to be looked at as a businessperson instead of a salesperson. Added benefits include better referrals, more introductions, and additional leads, simply because you will be able to get to new information more quickly (like the scoop that a new car dealership just signed a lease down the street from your existing prospects).

When you analyze the existing client lists as well as prospect lists of sales champions, you immediately see that the vast majority of them are very much focused on specific segments. How many segments to focus on will depend on the industry you are in and the type of product and service you are selling. In broadcast media, for example, teams might be asked to prospect so that a minimum of two-thirds of their lead list comes from a maximum of two segments, with each segment defined as narrowly as possible. Good examples for narrowly defined segments are "Online Education" instead of the very broad "Education" segment, or "Fertility Centers" as compared to the much broader "Healthcare" category. The remaining third of the lead list allows for more flexibility. Use categories and verticals to focus your prospecting efforts, but don't let them constrain you. If you see an opportunity outside of your core categories, maybe through a referral you received, go for it.

Sales aces also concentrate on a **limited** number of strategic targets. Although this might seem counterintuitive, especially for inexperienced salespeople, you will never make a better decision than spending more time on *better* and *fewer* accounts. If ever there is an area where "quality over quantity" or "less is more" wins, it is in B2B prospecting. As you will find out in subsequent chapters, once you have done the research on a lead, you have to decide if it deserves to be on your lead list or not. Once a lead makes the cut, don't change direction too quickly. It amazes me how much time salespeople are spending on identifying and evaluating leads, and how quickly they abandon a lead or an entire category only because they ran into one unexpected hurdle.

Let's say you have time to make one hundred outbound efforts a week, including cold calls, seed emails, and LinkedIn messages. What do you think will be more effective: reaching out to one hundred prospects once, or reaching out to ten prospects an average of ten times? Obviously the latter, because a limited number of well-researched leads allows for a much more customized approach and message for each individual prospect. With too many leads to connect with, salespeople get sloppy and revert back to generic messages, or don't give a potential good lead the attention it deserves. Having too many prospects on a lead list also tends to give salespeople a false sense of security, which again causes them to abandon good leads too early.

I wish I could give you an exact answer to the question of what the "right" number of prospects to target at any time is. But the answer really depends on too many variables, like type of industry and business, type of product or service, duration of sales cycle, price points, geographic area, even the experience level of salespeople and their existing client lists. Just as an example, a typical lead list for a mid-level salesperson in the New York media industry should probably be no longer than twenty to twenty-five prospects.

Even a segmented and limited list of leads still needs to be **prioritized**. You won't be able to give every one of your selected leads the same level of attention simply from a time-management and time-investment perspective. This does *not* mean that you should give bad leads a lower priority and leave them on your lead list. If a lead is not good enough and not worth your time, it shouldn't be on your lead list in the first place. Period. Don't justify to yourself that "you gave it a lower priority anyway" just so you can keep the lead on your list. If you start doing that, your lead list will quickly spiral out of control in terms of both volume and quality.

For example, your lead lists could be prioritized into the following three categories:

- **Dream Leads:** The top 10 percent of prospects that would be absolute game-changers and make your year, and potentially that of your company. Potential "whales" that make you jump out of bed and run to the office in the morning, because you are so excited that you found this lead that everyone else seems to have overlooked. Closing a dream lead is as good as it gets in our profession.

- **Excellent Leads:** The next level of prospects that look very similar to some of the company's best clients. You have success stories from their industry and it looks like a meeting with their main decision maker will be possible. Your research also indicates that the company has the funds to afford a medium- to large-scale proposal.
- **Solid Leads:** Potential "bread-and-butter" accounts that can generate part of your consistent base billing. Also includes prospects that—for different kinds of reasons—you feel very good about, but still need to gather more information on.

It is absolutely necessary to have a good mix of prospects instead of putting all your eggs in one basket. With a lead list of twenty-five prospects, a mix of three dream, ten excellent, and twelve solid leads seems like a good place to start.

Only focusing on the biggest prospects is a dangerous and risky game. I don't think it's a stretch to say that most people who end up in sales roles are optimists. And with that comes the danger that we overestimate closing ratios with dream leads. Pursuing dream leads has a lower probability of success, and this success—if it comes at all—usually takes longer to materialize. My advice is to have a lead list and plan in place that would get you to make your budget simply by closing leads you had prioritized as excellent and solid. And then, to consider dream leads to be the icing on the cake. If a dream lead closes, you have changed your year or even career. If it doesn't, you still make your number.

Most of the CRM systems on the market support lead prioritization, sometimes in fields called "Lead Rating." It is critical that you take advantage of this function; it keeps you on track and forces you to allocate your time most effectively.

THINK BIG

An account-list revenue analysis for a company that is providing customized solutions to other businesses will closely resemble the example shown in Figure 2.1. It plots the number of a company's clients on the x-axis, with the largest client on the left side and the smallest one all the way over to the right. As you can see, the company in this fictional example has about 230 clients. The corresponding annual revenue for each of these clients is plotted out on the y-axis. You will immediately notice the hockey-stick form of the graph, with the right side usually referred to as the "long tail." In our example, the company's largest client is spending around $10 million a year, the ninth largest around $4 million, the forty-sixth largest client around $500,000, and so on.

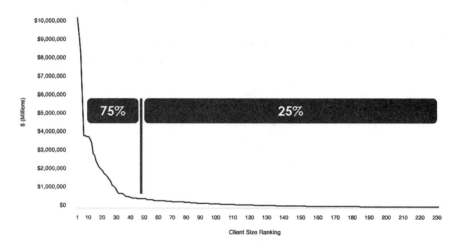

Figure 2.1: Typical Hockey-Stick Revenue Chart in B2B Sales-Focused Companies

An eye-opening exercise for new sellers is to have them guess how far they have to move to the right of the x-axis in order to get to the number of clients that together make up 75 percent of a company's revenue. The typical estimates are either very close to the middle of the graph, or even further to the right. You need a lot of accounts to get to three-quarters of the company's total revenue, the thinking goes. And, of course, that couldn't be further from the truth. It usually only takes the revenue of about 15 to 25 percent (in our example, 18 percent) of the total number of clients to generate 75 percent of a company's total revenue.

These accounts are commonly referred to as Key Accounts: the clients that financially contribute the most to a company's revenue in the short and long term, with annual renewal rates much higher than smaller accounts. In fact, there is usually a direct correlation between a client's investment level with a company and the renewal rate. Key Accounts are the clients that are looking for deeper and more integrated strategic partnerships, which typically result in the company offering more and more services. Key Accounts also look good in a case study, which helps to attract other large companies.

The accounts on the right side of the chart, on the other hand, not only contribute little revenue; the return on a salesperson's time investment is also much lower. Small clients are certainly as demanding as larger ones, but also are usually less reliable when it comes to payment and overall usually less satisfied, resulting in the already mentioned lower renewal rates.

So why are salespeople going after these small accounts? The blunt truth is because they don't know how to prospect or don't have the confidence to engage with larger leads. The successful salesperson is the one who knows how to play on the left side of the chart. That's where careers are being made and large commission checks earned. Segmenting, limiting, and prioritizing your prospect lists is the best possible start to get you there. This doesn't mean that every new business account has to and can become a Key Account in the first year. It sometimes takes a few years to grow an account to that level. But they should have the *potential* of becoming a Key Account within a certain period (which can differ by industry, although three years is probably realistic).

PROSPECTING PROCESS

The prospecting process encompasses two steps, which we will cover in the next three chapters:

1. Identifying leads: the process of generating lists of potential prospects that initially look attractive.
2. Efficiently evaluating and researching each one of these prospects based on a predetermined set of criteria.

Our goal for the first step is to find a larger number of leads. In the second step, we can narrow down the lead list further by using a process of elimination.

3

ALL GLORY COMES FROM DARING TO BEGIN

ompared to the other tactical steps in the sales process, prospecting provides the rare opportunity to ask yourself big-picture questions and make strategic decisions. Since you're making key strategic decisions that will have a long-term impact on your performance, you should stay in close contact with your sales manager throughout the process. There is a lot of information you might not have access to, and your manager's knowledge and experience will prove invaluable in keeping you on track. There would be no way, for example, for you to know your company's different closing ratios in specific business segments, with your goal of course being to focus on the ones where the company has seen higher numbers. Your manager can also immediately tell you which segments are already well covered by other salespeople on your team. Excellent sales managers view supporting their sales force during the prospecting phase as essential, so take advantage of their expertise.

CREATING IDEAL PROSPECT PROFILES

In some sales positions, especially at larger companies, leads are provided by the marketing or lead-generation department. However, at most small- and medium-sized businesses, salespeople are expected to find their own leads. And that can be pretty overwhelming, especially if you are new to it. Meanwhile, the thirty-year veteran in the cubicle next to you is letting you know that, "All the good leads are already taken, but good luck to you!"

That sales veteran, of course, is flat-out wrong, no matter the industry you are in. Most likely, he himself just forgot how to prospect. Think about all the new businesses that are being started across the country every year or the decision makers who leave their positions, opening the door for successors with potentially very different views about their vendors and partners. Yes, the opportunities are there. You just need to follow the process and find them.

The most effective salespeople start by looking at their company's best current customers:

- What are their characteristics?
- Which customer segments are dominant? Which industries? Which geographic territories? What type of business?
- In what stage of a typical life cycle of a business are they? Are they start-ups? Are they market leaders?
- Why are they using us and not our competitors?
- What are the different closing ratios per segment?
- For what customer segments do we have the best case studies?

You have a much greater chance of closing new business by focusing on business segments with which the company is already seeing success. It will be much easier to confidently position yourself and your company as experts, and it will also be likely that prospects will have heard of some of the customer names you are mentioning, which further increases your credibility.

BIRDS OF A FEATHER FLOCK TOGETHER

But don't companies prefer to deal with partners who do *not* offer similar services to too many of their competitors? To use the media industry as an example: Would a personal injury lawyer be more inclined to sign an advertising contract with a TV station that is *not* airing ads from another personal injury lawyer, with the salesperson's positioning being that the lawyer would stand out much more and could really dominate the space? Or could this law firm be persuaded more easily by a list of ten other personal injury law firms that have been seeing great results and became long-term advertisers of that TV station? In my experience, nineteen out of twenty times the latter is a more effective strategy. Just check your Sunday newspaper's sports section, with one car dealership advertisement next to the other, and you'll understand what I mean. There are many reasons for this tactic, one of which is that it gives the buyers cover in case the chosen solution doesn't deliver the expected results. It minimizes their risk. Let's say, in our example, the advertising campaign didn't generate the desired results. It's much easier and safer to explain this to the powers that be by saying the strategy followed what many of the competitors were already successfully doing. Something else must have been the reason for the poor results.

NEW BUSINESS TRENDS LEAD TO NEW PROSPECTING OPPORTUNITIES

Changes in certain business segments usually open up new opportunities for companies. Just look what happened to many industries during the coronavirus crisis. Sales champions took advantage of these changes and shifted their prospecting focus to categories that benefited from the economic turmoil. They targeted emerging categories like online education, faith-based websites and apps, or home fitness equipment.

The coronavirus pandemic also turned out to be a geographic equalizer for sales forces that had been prospecting mostly in their immediate surroundings. Most of them were used to setting up in-person meetings with their prospects. Since those were no longer possible, and all calls—no matter if the client was located in-market or far away—were done through video anyway, flexible salespeople expanded their geographic view and focused on new, previously less heavily targeted territories.

It is always an effective strategy to identify segments that are in the beginning stages of a growth spurt. This allows you to participate in the early success that companies in these segments are seeing, and positions you to expand your prospecting focus when new players enter the segments.

GENERATING LEAD LISTS

Remember while you are generating your lists that not all of the leads have to be good at this point. In a second step, we will filter out the ones that we don't want to focus on further. Figure 3.1 provides an overview of different lead sources you can focus on.

Referrals

If you start a career as a real estate broker, one of the first things you are advised is to call every family member and every friend you have—childhood friends, college friends, work friends, new friends—and ask them if they are in the market for a house or condo or know someone who is. Smart thinking! Too bad that with the exception of a handful of industries, very few are doing this strategically and consistently. Most people completely underestimate how large their personal network actually is. Just add up the LinkedIn connections of all your family members and all your friends. I guarantee you it is sizable.

Some of the best deals I was part of started with client or prospect referrals. Clients love to help, but without you actively asking them for referrals you will be missing out on great opportunities. Sometimes prospects are an even better source than clients, especially right after the

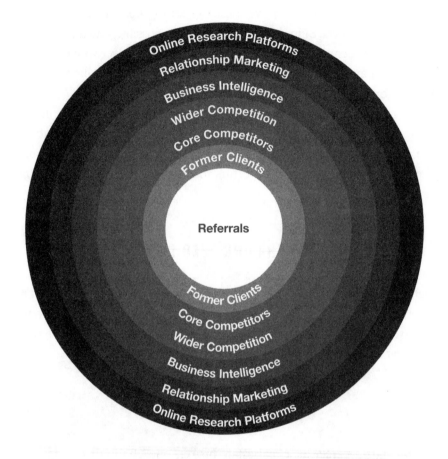

Figure 3.1: Different Lead Source Categories

moment they told you they can't sign off on a proposal you just presented. They will want to let you down easy and will try their best to assist you. The following prompt is a good start:

"I'm disappointed that this didn't work out this time. But now that you have gotten to know me and our company better, can you think of anyone else I might be able to help?"

Your existing customers may also have other divisions or brands that might be a good fit for whatever you are offering. This is another way to pick up leads very easily.

Former Clients

For the new salesperson who just joined a company, contacting old customers—companies that used to be clients but are no longer—is a no-brainer. Again, however, few people actually do it. They are afraid that if the solution provided the last time wasn't satisfactory, this former client is no longer interested in talking to them. What they are forgetting is that new salespeople also have full "deniability" in a sense that they were not part of the problem—if there was one—the first time around. For instance, you could say:

"I am sorry to hear that happened. But we have a new team in place here, myself included, with a lot of experience and many new ideas that are getting our clients results. I would love to come in and show you a few case studies, including results we generated for other companies in your category. Sound fair?"

How do you know what the former client thinks? How do you know what the person will say? You won't know until you make the call. Ask your manager to pull you a report from your CRM system and add old customers who are no longer buying from the company to your lead list. You are missing a huge opportunity if you don't.

Core Competitors

Core competitors and their client lists are your next source of prospects. Core competitors are companies that provide a very similar service to what your company provides. Assuming you are offering competitive solutions, your conversion ratios with these prospects (into meetings and sales) will be higher than average. These companies are already sold on what you sell; they are just buying it from someone else. Game on! We will cover different positioning and sales tactics for this situation later in chapter fifteen, but the great news here is that someone else already educated the prospect on the *why* of your product or service.

If you are selling audio advertising, for example, calling on a company that has already seen success using this medium means that you don't have to convince the decision makers on the power of audio and sound. You only have to convince them that your idea, your brand, and your firm are a better fit for them compared to what they are currently using.

Different industries use various competitive monitoring databases. Staying with our gold-digging analogy from chapter two, these are the equivalent of metal detectors. Many media companies use tools like Media Monitors, which allow you to pull all the advertisers that bought time on competitive media during a preselected time period. If you sell advertising for a local TV station in Boston, you can easily select all the other TV stations in the Boston market and, within seconds, receive a list of all their advertisers.

The only cautionary advice with this prospecting tactic is that if you are able to "steal" an account from your competitor, then your competitor will also try to do the same to you. This happens in every industry—it's the day-to-day blocking and tackling in sales. You can never take an account for granted.

Expanded Competitive View

Continue to widen the circle by monitoring companies that might not offer a similar product or service, but are either addressing a comparable need a prospect is facing, or are competing for the same budget. For example, an advertiser in Boston naturally has many other advertising options than just local TV stations. TV salespeople should therefore start a list of advertisers they find by monitoring newspaper, radio, outdoor, direct mail, magazine, or any form of digital advertising, even in-store advertising they uncover through strategic prospecting initiatives. Once they actually connect with these prospects, they will have to take the additional step of selling the medium (in this case TV) first. Only once they've received buy-in will they move on to their actual concept and solution.

One of the most important determinations you have to make during the prospecting phase is to establish whether a prospect will have the funds to afford your offerings. Expanding your competitive view allows you to easily do this by monitoring how much money is being spent on whatever they are currently buying from other solution providers in the space. There are many monitoring tools available to assist in searching these competitive platforms for leads. Databases like Kantar or Miller Kaplan's X-Ray are examples used in the media space, with both providing spending data of advertisers across several marketing platforms.

Business Intelligence

While competitive monitoring and databases are very effective and efficient ways to prospect, you need to understand that they can only report on activities that have already happened. To use our TV example, you will be able to see what companies advertised on which TV stations or other media outlets in the past week, or month, or year, depending on the time horizon you select.

It certainly is possible to project from past business behavior into the future. Think about a company that buys business travel solutions in the exact same week as their corporate off-site meeting every year. But to really predict future business opportunities, a salesperson needs to go a step further and stay informed about trends and other company developments in their core focus segments.

For instance, consider a grocery store chain that is active only in the Northeast and decides to expand into California and Arizona. Or a start-up that hasn't launched yet, but has received millions of dollars in funding. Or a new brand launched by an established player. You would not be able to find these prospects in a monitoring database. But you can find out about this type of news by reading trade or business magazines, by talking to other people in the category, even by talking to your competitors (yes, developing connections with people active in your industry is never a bad idea!). A great platform where you can learn about start-ups that have recently received funding is CrunchBase.

Networking

Relationship marketing/networking is not only a great way to get introductions and set up new business meetings, it is also a great way to find out about emerging trends in a particular industry (e.g., how market shares have been shifting or any new entrants into the field). Conventions and trade shows in the marketing world like FinCon, CES, South by Southwest, and the Advertising Festival in Cannes are great examples of events with thousands of participants that offer numerous opportunities to network. Some of them can be costly, but that's usually more the case for exhibitors than regular attendees. Even if the real decision makers typically will not be physically present on the exhibit floor, walking the aisles and talking to people at the booths of potential leads can be an efficient and effective way to prospect. More locally, business journals like *Crain's Business* host and publish business events. Many of them are free, and the ones that are not are often worth the investment.

It is also easier than ever to actively join networking groups. Some are being hosted regularly as video chats on Zoom, while others meet in person. And companies like Chief, a private network focused on connecting and supporting female leaders, have made a prospering business out of it.

The important thing about relationship marketing is that you fully commit to it. You will be spending money and time on it, so you need to have a plan. It takes the right preparation, focus, and effort, and it certainly can be exhausting, but it has a great multiplier effect. Jeffrey Gitomer describes networking as "building a people resource bank that pays interest and dividends that compound annually for as long as you are alive." People will pick up quickly on the fact that you are just there to make a quick buck, so don't approach it in an aggressive, sales-driven manner. Sales champions understand that networking is about nurturing long-term relationships.

Online Research Platforms

Expand your search further by using additional resources available to the B2B salesperson. A great example is the Book of Lists, which local business journals like *Crain's Business* publish once a year. The Book of Lists ranks companies in different industries by size. You want to know the biggest banks in your market? The fastest-growing companies? The largest privately held companies? The Book of Lists includes them all. They come in both online and printed formats.

Online research platforms like Winmo, Hoover's, or LimeLeads allow you to create customized lead lists based on user-defined criteria. You can filter by location, revenue, industry, type of business, and other parameters. We will cover LinkedIn and how to use it to connect with prospects in a later chapter. But it is worth mentioning LinkedIn's Sales Navigator platform as a great prospecting tool here. Its "search for leads" and "search for accounts" functionality is invaluable. Sales Navigator requires an annual fee, but—at the risk of sounding like a LinkedIn salesperson—the investment will be worth it many times over.

Needless to say, Google searches can also help you generate lead lists. Along with helping you find leads, the results also allow you to find more detailed information about certain business segments and their players.

Remember, though, when you're using online research platforms, they allow you to pull thousands of companies and potential prospects. Of course, that's not a bad thing, except that it can become overwhelming quickly. Many times, it is not easy to establish if a particular prospect is worth pursuing. This is the main reason why, in Figure 3.1, online research platforms fall into the widest prospecting circle. The inner circles allow for comparatively much more targeted prospecting.

4

CREATING QUALIFIED LEAD LISTS

A t this point in the sales process you should have generated lists of leads from different sources. These should all be prospects that, at first glance, look promising to you. You absolutely must keep track of the lead source for each of these prospects. Did you find them because they are doing business with a competitor? Did they pop up in a Google search? Did someone tell you about a new company that just got start-up funding but hasn't launched yet? Don't lose this information; it will keep you on course and prevent the number of leads that originate in the outer circles of our chart (e.g., Google searches) from getting out of control. Remember, you want to have a good mix of leads, and lead source is an important part of determining lead quality.

YOUR MANAGER AS YOUR ALLY

Before you start evaluating and researching every one of your leads, you should show your initial lead list to your manager. Unless they are newly hired, your manager should be in an ideal position to review your suggestions with you and—without your spending time doing further research on them—eliminate the ones that you shouldn't contact for whatever reason. Don't underestimate how much time this extra step will save you. I mentioned earlier that prospecting is one of the most strategic activities in the entire sales process. You want to have your manager as your partner here. They will know whether a prospect has a terrible payment history in the market, has already been called on by someone else on your team, or is a buyer whose spouse works with your main competitor.

Good managers also consider finding leads part of their job, and they assign these leads to their salespeople. However, don't assume that every lead from your manager is automatically a great prospect. Always ask where the lead came from. You still have to research and determine if that particular prospect is worth your time. And if you determine you don't want to focus on a particular lead from management, don't be afraid to speak up and let your manager know.

Only after you review your initial list with your manager do you check your CRM system to find out which of the prospects you found are available to be called on, which ones are already actively being pursued by a teammate, and which ones are already a client. A word of caution here: instead of just giving up on a lead that has met with or even been pitched to by someone on your team, challenge your manager to find out how much activity there really has been with a prospect. Maybe the last proposal the prospect saw was a while ago. Maybe the buyer has been called on for years, but it never resulted in a sale. Maybe it's time for a change.

NARROWING DOWN YOUR LEAD LIST

By now, you have started to reduce your extensive lead list to your best prospects, the ones with whom you will actually try to connect. In sticking with our gold-nugget prospecting analogy, we are separating gold from black sand. We will do that by running each lead through several filters.

Is your product or service right for the prospect's business and its customers? We want to focus on prospects that are a perfect fit for the solutions we offer. For example, a furniture manufacturer specializing in high-end bedroom furniture should target a high-end furniture retail store whose customers are wealthy homeowners, instead of trying to sell to a budget furniture outlet. A radio station whose audience is young and skews female might identify a car brand targeting female millennials as a potential advertiser. Companies like Nielsen offer indexes for thousands of different items that allow you to determine how close of an audience match there is. In our example, we could have easily determined that both the radio station's audience and the car brand's buyers are high-indexing with young women. Station and car brand would therefore be a good match for each other.

A company's social media channels, advertising creative, and even financial statements can give you a good idea about its positioning and core customers. Also, the About the Company section of a prospect's website can provide you with valuable information.

Do you have access to key decision makers?

In many industries, encountering some type of middle party is very common. Think about consultants who manage the selection of advertising agencies for larger companies, or media agencies that handle the media buying of marketers. In an ideal scenario, the prospects you are researching operate without such middle parties, which results in decision makers meeting with their partners and vendors directly. Or consider this from a geographic perspective. If you are working in an industry that involves selling complex solutions that take several in-person meetings to develop, present, and sell, you would have easier and more access if the decision maker were based in your area.

However, don't get stuck on the notion that there is only one key decision maker. Several studies conducted in the last decade have confirmed an increase in "consensus requirement" within medium-sized and larger companies. Even very senior decision makers are less and less likely to go out on a limb for a supplier on a big purchase decision, at least not on their own. While there is still a lot to be said for the old sales adage of "start at the top and work your way down," there are many other levels that can offer you entry points into a qualified prospect. Often, the only way to get in the door with a key buyer is by first laying the groundwork with other stakeholders within the company. These can be lower-level influencers who are reporting to the senior executive level, whose trust needs to be earned first. When it's time to make a big purchasing choice, decision makers want to ensure they have the backing, support, and buy-in from their team.

Will the prospect be able to adequately fund a potential solution by your company?

In many industries it is possible to determine how much a prospect is currently spending on services similar to the ones you are offering. A company like Kantar, for example, allows you to access spending data for different kinds of media (outdoor, TV, radio, print, etc.) to determine the budget sizes of prospects.

Size of the company, of course, plays a big role here. Many services and databases provide revenue estimates for companies. Take advantage of them. But margins and price points are important as well. For example, if you are a healthcare marketing agency that specializes in increasing the number of patients for doctors' offices, you will find that it is easier to see a return on marketing investment for offices that are fully focused on elective procedures with high price points, like plastic surgery or LASIK eye surgery. That's because the number of new patients your marketing campaign needs to deliver for a higher-priced procedure will be less. It will be much harder for most primary-care physicians whose campaigns need to attract many patients to achieve a similar return on investment (ROI).

KNOWLEDGE IS POWER

As you research your prospects, make sure you are saving and keeping the information you uncover for each of the prospects that make your final lead list. In the next section ("Connect") we will be covering "Relevant Business Reasons" (RBRs), with which we will approach prospects by phone, email, and other channels. To come up with the most effective RBRs, we will need to access the most important intelligence you uncovered during the prospecting phase. Prospecting is the best prep work to ensure you say the right things to a prospect once you start a dialogue with them.

Today, most companies require their salespeople to enter their leads into their CRM system to make them easily trackable. Beyond that, you need to develop a system to capture the information you uncover during your prospecting work, specifically what you deem necessary for later use. This includes articles you found about the company, spending reports, and potentially even organizational charts, financial statements, and marketing creative.

5

DEVELOPING YOUR PROSPECTING SYSTEM

You started with a longer list of leads that you identified during your different prospecting tactics, then narrowed it down by researching and evaluating them using our three filters. The end result is a segmented, limited, and prioritized lead list.

Successful salespeople know exactly which prospects they are pursuing at any time, and all the reasons why they are investing time in them. There is nothing vague about their leads. If you wake up sales champions in the middle of the night, they will be able to recite all of their top leads. There is also nothing vague about their prospecting systems. Sales aces develop a system that they follow religiously and capture the most important information on each of their prospects to have at their fingertips when they start to reach out to them. They understand that they won't be able to pull up the information from memory, especially once they start to juggle many different prospects and are at different stages of outreach for each of them.

PREPARATION IS GOOD, EFFICIENT PREPARATION IS BETTER

Abraham Lincoln said that if he had eight hours to chop down a tree, he'd spend the first six of them sharpening the ax. In general, this approach describes how sales champions approach prospecting. When they see a potentially good prospect, they don't just pick up the phone and call with a generic message. They spend time to research and evaluate, customize an RBR, decide on a plan of attack, and then execute. But how much time should be spent on this preparatory work?

Over-preparation in sales is as common as under-preparation. There is no reason to precede every call with hours of research worthy of a college assignment. At this point in the sales process, the extent of your research should be enough to:

- determine if, based on the different filters you are applying (product and audience match, access to decision makers, budget), the prospect should have a place on your lead list.
- allow you to develop a customized RBR.
- identify key decision makers or decision influencers at the company and their contact information.

You can usually do all that pretty quickly. I see far too many sales-people getting lost in the details, going down too many rabbit holes when doing Google searches on a prospect. Most salespeople enjoy doing this type of research—or, to be more specific, they enjoy it more than cold calling. As a result, they risk spending too much time finding and validating information, and not enough time setting up new face-to-face business meetings. If you would bill yourself for the time you will be spending researching a prospect, would it be worth your investment?

STRATEGIC PROSPECTING

Effective salespeople are always alert and looking out for leads. You might be noticing leads at night while watching TV, or during the day in the car on the way to a sales call. Of course you want to capture these. But don't mistake this for "strategic prospecting."

Strategic prospecting means setting aside time in your calendar and doing all the prospecting tasks we just covered—and, equally important, doing them consistently. I see many sales pros block out Friday afternoons to do this kind of work. Their reasoning is that at the end of the week, they had already put enough time into setting up new business meetings and wanted to end the week with work that would motivate them for the following week. And what better way to do that than finding a new prospect everyone else has overlooked? Monday can't come fast enough. In the end, it doesn't really matter which day of the week you make these appointments with yourself; just don't schedule them in the middle of the prime selling hours.

DON'T GIVE UP TOO EARLY

One of the biggest differences between experienced sales champions and sales rookies is their focus on their lead lists. Rookies easily get frustrated when they are not able to get in the door with their prospects. They hear one objection from a person at the company they are reaching out to—maybe even a lower-level employee—and out the window the lead goes. We'll just replace it with a new one, right? Wrong! Effective salespeople are more patient and remind themselves that often the best prospects are the toughest ones to crack. They stay laser-focused on finding ways to meet with prospects in whom they have invested a good amount of research time. If they weren't convinced the prospect is worth their time, the prospect wouldn't be on their lead list in the first place. This applies especially to dream leads. Some of the best deals that I have witnessed took a while to materialize, including several failed attempts to set up meetings with decision makers at the beginning of the sales process.

CASE STUDY: MEET REBECCA GYMS

Rebecca Gyms is a fictional gym that will accompany us for the rest of the book so we can put the sales strategies and tactics introduced into practice, and to make scripts, objections, and proposals that follow later in the book more realistic and easier to follow.

Assume you are part of the advertising sales force of a family-owned local media company based in New York that operates local magazines, radio stations, and digital platforms. That company is—very creatively—called NYC Media, and its platforms reach more than five million people in the tristate area.

You saw a job posting for a Rebecca Gyms New York district manager in New York's *Crain's Business* magazine. The name of the company didn't ring a bell, which led you to believe that Rebecca Gyms was either a new brand of an existing gym provider (similar to how Equinox Gyms started Blink Fitness), a new fitness start-up, or an existing regional gym brand located in a different geographic area of the country trying to expand into the Northeast.

A quick Google search confirmed the latter. Rebecca Gyms is a company based in San Diego, with 103 locations on the West Coast, in California, Oregon, and Washington. A Wikipedia entry shows that it is a privately owned company, founded in 1994, and still run by founder and CEO Rebecca Miller.

You check with your sales manager to find out if she has ever heard of the company or whether she knows if anyone on the team has already reached out. She didn't think so. You check Salesforce and confirm that there has not been any activity with this account. Since NYC Media doesn't operate media properties on the West Coast, this doesn't come as a surprise.

You access Rebecca Gyms' website and start reading the About the Company section, where you not only see the number of locations by state, but also their work with charities (mostly UNICEF and the Obesity Action Coalition) and their mission statement: "To provide strong and confident women with a workout place they can call their own." All of their 103 centers are owned and operated by the company. They don't seem to offer franchising opportunities.

All the images shown on the homepage are of women of different ages—between 25 and 50 years old—and different ethnicities. Their current TV spot promoting their West Coast locations can be viewed on the homepage. The thirty-second spot uses the tagline "Fitness That Fits Women," shows several women working out together, and ends with the offer to "come with a friend, and you'll both receive 50 percent off for the first six months."

In the Executive Team section (a subsection of About the Company), you not only get introduced to Rebecca Miller, but also to Chief Financial Officer Thomas Miller (going off his picture, potentially Rebecca's son), Chief Fitness Manager Lucy Borgen, Chief Marketing Officer Tracy Ranner, and Chief Membership Officer Frank Rosen. Unfortunately, their email addresses are not included in their bios, so you go to hunter.io and determine their email addresses are the first letter of their first name combined with their full last name, then @rebecca gyms.com. You assume from the geographic locations of their gyms that the entire C-suite is based in San Diego. You go to LinkedIn to determine if you have any mutual connections, but since Rebecca Gyms is at this point a West Coast–oriented company, you don't.

Quick Google and Winmo searches don't result in any hits for advertising agencies working with Rebecca Gyms. You therefore make the assumption that the company's marketing team is working directly with media outlets on its marketing campaigns, and make a note to confirm this once you are face to face with a prospect there. Google did uncover an interesting interview *Advertising Age* conducted with CMO Tracy Ranner three months ago.

To find out more about its advertising expenditure, you run a Kantar report that shows Rebecca Gyms' media mix as:

- $4.9m broadcast TV advertising (54%)
- $2.2m radio advertising (25%)
- $1.1m outdoor advertising (12%)
- $0.8m newspaper advertising (9%)

You run a Media Monitors report on the company's western markets and notice that the radio stations bought most frequently are female-skewing Adult Contemporary and Top 40 radio stations, and that on the TV side, Rebecca Gyms seems to have loyalty to local NBC affiliates. The company is running full-page ads in one local newspaper per market. When listening to its radio commercial you make a note that the creative follows the audio of their TV spot, but question whether that is the most effective way to use the medium.

A query on Sponsor United shows that Rebecca Gyms is an in-stadium sponsor of the Los Angeles Dodgers, a strange choice for a 100 percent female-oriented company.

Last, you check out the company's Instagram and Twitter channels. With 14,000 Twitter followers and 51,000 Instagram followers, it seems that Rebecca Gyms' social media following is below average when compared to other similarly sized fitness centers. A quick scroll through the most recent posts shows a broad mix of topics, from healthy eating to a "trainer of the week" feature.

Throughout this process, you are mentally running the information you are gathering through our three filters:

Is NYC Media's product or service right for Rebecca Gyms' business and its customers?

Yes! Clearly, the company is trying to reach middle-aged females. NYC Media is operating several female-skewing radio stations in New York as well as a health-oriented digital platform with an 80 percent female audience.

Do you have access to Rebecca Gyms' key decision makers?

Yes! It doesn't seem that the company is using third-party consultants or agencies for its media buys. You have the names and email addresses of all C-suite members and are confident a LinkedIn search will uncover more potential contacts. The fact that all of them seem to be located on the West Coast is certainly not ideal, but you should be able to set up a face-to-face video call. Hopefully they are making progress hiring a locally-based district manager who you could also meet in person.

Will Rebecca Gyms be able to adequately fund a potential solution by NYC Media?

Yes! Based on the Kantar and Media Monitors information, you believe this could be a sizable account once the company launches on the East Coast.

You spent exactly thirty-four minutes doing this research, and now have determined that the prospect Rebecca Gyms is worth your time. As a result, you open the lead in Salesforce. You upload all the reports you just pulled to the Rebecca Gyms account and add notes about all the other relevant information you uncovered. You will need these in the next steps of the sales process.

You are convinced this is a good lead and you're pumped! It's time to plan and kick off your marketing campaign to set up a video call with them.

CONNECT

6

SETTING UP FACE-TO-FACE MEETINGS

N ow that you've identified and evaluated your leads and built a segmented, limited, and prioritized prospect list, it's time to move on to what many consider to be the most difficult task of the entire sales process: connecting with the prospect. You can do this by using several different channels, which usually work in tandem:

- phone
- email
- LinkedIn and other social media networks
- in person

Depending on your industry, product, service, and type of prospect you are reaching out to, you will typically try to accomplish one of four core connecting objectives:

- Scheduling a face-to-face meeting, either in person or through a video call.

- Increasing awareness of your company and yourself with the prospect. This is especially important for salespeople who work for lesser-known companies or new ventures.
- Gathering additional information about the prospect. This is relevant in industries selling to customers for which few data points are available and can be found during the prospecting phase (e.g., companies that sell to very small businesses).
- Closing a deal. Many industries are driven much more by quantity than quality (e.g., an industry selling products that are sold at a low price point) and are therefore focused on getting a deal done on the first outreach.

Covering all of these objectives would go beyond the scope of this book. We will focus mostly on achieving the first goal (setting up a face-to-face meeting with the prospect) and will touch on the second one (increasing awareness), especially during chapter eleven on social selling and leaving voicemails.

NOT COLD CALLING AGAIN!

Of the different ways to connect with a prospect, approaching by phone—commonly referred to as cold calling—is surrounded by the most stigma and is probably the main reason people shy away from a career in sales. The typical sales stereotype portrayed in movies like *The Wolf of Wall Street* or *Glengarry Glen Ross* and even in TV shows like *Seinfeld* ("Hello, Mr. Farneman! You wanna buy a computer? No? Why not?") is that of sleazy salespeople trying to trick their way in the door with a prospect. That is how most people who have never worked in a B2B sales role imagine the day-to-day routine of a typical salesperson.

Who can blame them? Searching for synonyms for the term "cold calling" on Google and Thesaurus.com will suggest the following four expressions: "hard sell," "sales call," "spam," and "spit." Yes, it says "spit"! Over the years, companies have tried to give it different names—"proactive calling," "moneymaking calling," and "making marketing calls" is just a short list of these rebranding efforts, none of which ever really stuck. It's less about the label than the activity itself, anyway. And let's face it, that activity sucks! Over the years, I have met very few people who claimed to enjoy cold calling, and if someone did, I walked away every single time not believing one word.

To be clear, under the term "cold calling" we mean calling someone who is not expecting your call in order to initiate a sales conversation and a future client relationship. What makes it "cold" is that the recipient of your call is not expecting it. Instead, you are interrupting the person's day, and that interruption typically results in some type of initial resistance and potentially a negative response. That's what makes cold calling so hard.

But here is the key point: you don't have to enjoy cold calling to become good at it. You just have to commit to it and do it. And when you think about it, cold calling typically doesn't make up more than 10 to 20 percent of a typical workweek. So what if you don't love these cold-calling hours? As long as the calls help you enjoy the other 80 to 90 percent of the week, you should be able to manage. Show me a job that is 100 percent perfect all the time. It doesn't exist!

HITTING YOUR FIRST SALES SERVE

As a former tennis player, I see several similarities between cold calling in an office (or wherever you prefer to do it) and starting a new point on a tennis court, which you do by hitting a first serve. The serve is the one shot in tennis that your opponents cannot influence. You can hit a flat serve, a kick serve, or a topspin serve. You can mix up the speed of the serve. It's all completely up to the server. Only after the player on the other side of the net returns the serve does the rally begin. And at that point, your next shot will be influenced by how your opponent reacted.

This is very similar to the situation you are facing when reaching out to a new prospect. It is entirely up to you what you say or write, at least initially. So make it count. "I want to come in and tell you how great my company is" or some other product dump will not do and is more akin to double faulting in tennis. Depending on what type of reaction and answer you get from the prospect to your opening, you decide what type of question to follow up with to turn the call into a conversation, or the sales equivalent of a rally in tennis.

A typical training session in tennis is mostly spent on practicing ground strokes, forehands, and backhands, as well as working on the net game, hitting volleys and overheads. And maybe, only maybe, there will be five minutes left at the end of the training session to hit some serves. It is by far the most under-practiced shot in the game. In fact, players who actually did heavily focus on it during practice throughout their careers like Pete Sampras or Boris Becker, were able to dominate the game by excelling with exactly this shot. Because salespeople don't enjoy cold calling, they don't like to practice cold calling, when it is probably the one activity in sales that allows you to improve your sales performance very quickly, whether by role-playing, reviewing scripts and talking points, and practicing how to handle objections.

QUALIFYING PROSPECTS ON WARM CALLS

In the sales world you will sometimes come across the term "warm calling." It's commonly understood as the prospect having indicated some type of initial interest, such as filling out a form on your company's website, or actively calling in to be connected to the sales department. Of course, gathering information and immediately qualifying the prospect will become the primary objective of such a call. Without dwelling too much on this particular scenario, let me stress the significance of having the confidence to ask fact-based questions on this initial call, like the budget they have available right now, so you avoid wasting time setting up face-to-face meetings with unqualified prospects.

ONE COLD-CALL OBJECTIVE

If you work in an industry where the objective of a cold call is to set up a face-to-face meeting, it's essential to set exactly that as your bar of success before you pick up the phone and dial. It's very simple: if you schedule a meeting—in person or on video—your cold call was a success; if you don't, it was not. If your one and only goal is to set up a face-to-face meeting, it's also important to understand what is *not* a goal. It's *not* your goal to conduct a thorough needs analysis with your prospect over the phone. It's *not* your goal to keep your prospect on the phone longer, just to "make friends." It's *not* your goal to sell your solution. You would think this is all pretty straightforward, but it's not. Some salespeople are trying to convince themselves that a call that didn't result in a meeting was still a "win."

"She didn't give me the meeting, but was really interested in what I had to say."

"I really connected with him on a personal level. He has young kids and so do I. They are not ready yet from a business perspective, but it was a good start."

It could be a good start, but justifying calls that fall short of your goal like that is a very slippery slope that can result in a very successful week of cold calling (at least in your eyes), yet no face-to-face meetings with new business prospects. Be strict about sticking to your objective.

7

THE THREE COLD-CALLING SUCCESS FACTORS

To maximize your chances of scheduling face-to-face meetings with new business prospects, you will need to excel in three areas:

- Attitude, Energy, and Tonality
- Outreach System
- Relevant Business Reason

In sales trainings, I often ask the group which one of these three areas they think is the most important. The answer is almost always the same: the vast majority thinks the RBR is the difference maker, following the notion that *what* you say is more important for a successful cold call than *how* you say it and *how often* you say it. If they only had some magic words or phrases, their prospects would automatically relent and everything would fall into place. Unfortunately (or fortunately, depending how you look at it), it doesn't work like that. There is no secret cold-calling language that—once you learn it—will change your life, even if many books, videos, and seminars promise it.

Becoming an excellent cold caller means being excellent in all three of the mentioned areas, which are all equally important. You can't win by being great in two areas and very weak in the third one. You won't get the meeting if you have the best and most customized RBR but sound like a thirteen-year-old on the phone. You can have the most structured approach, but may still fail because of what you are saying to the buyer. You can have the best attitude and all the energy in the world, but without a system to keep track of your phone conversations, you won't succeed. Yes, that means that more than half of your cold-calling success will depend on things other than *what* you are actually saying!

ATTITUDE, ENERGY, AND TONALITY

Nothing is worse than a salesperson who sounds like a salesperson. I am not even talking about the actual words you are using. We will get to these when we cover good RBRs. I am talking about *how* you sound, including the tone of your voice, your speech patterns and pace, and your modulation. Making sure your tonality matches the words you are using is essential to coming across not like a telemarketer, but as the business resource your future partners are looking for. While this will sound a little different for every salesperson, and while there are certainly many different speaking styles that can be successful, Jeb Blount, in his book *Fanatical Prospecting*, does an excellent job summarizing what demonstrates this kind of businesslike and confident demeanor on the phone:

- Speaking with normal inflection and a deeper pitch is more effective than speaking with a high pitched voice.
- Appropriate voice modulation with emotional emphasis on the right words and phrases is more effective than speaking really loudly, or really softly, throughout the phone call.

- Speaking at a relaxed pace, using appropriate pauses, is more effective than speaking too fast.
- Coming across in a friendly tone, with a smile in your voice, will get you further than a tense or defensive tone of voice.
- Direct speech that gets right to the point will generate better results than a nervous tone of voice with too many filler words, like "um"s or "uh"s.

We already spent some time on the necessary attitude and confidence of sales champions in the Commit section. While it applies throughout the entire sales process, these intangibles are probably most important during the Connect phase. The last thing anyone wants is to do business with someone who comes across as phlegmatic. If prospects sense fear, nervousness, or lack of energy, they will shut you down within ten seconds. Energy sells, because it conveys enthusiasm and confidence—in the product or service you are selling, and in yourself as a businessperson. Of course, too much energy and too much confidence can backfire, as you run the risk of being perceived as too pushy.

Be "On" and Prepared

Once you dial the number, you need to be "on." I have seen sales aces use different tactics that help them ensure a consistently high level of energy, like standing up or at least sitting up straight when making cold calls, using headsets to be able to "talk" with both hands and take notes more easily, or actively trying to put a smile on their face when they start the call, "transferring" the smile to their voice.

One of the biggest energy and confidence boosts you can get is simply being prepared. Think back to your high school or college days and what a difference it made when you chose to study hard and, as a result, knew all the facts on the day of the test. Your energy and confidence levels were higher simply because of your preparedness. Knowing your talking points, anticipating potential objections, doing your research on the prospect, maybe even role-playing an important call to one of your dream leads with your manager or a coworker, will all boost your confidence. That confidence will come across on the call.

Ride the Wave

The biggest energy boost you will feel is right after you have set up a meeting with a new prospect. Your adrenaline is flowing, and your confidence level will be up. Don't stop now. Your chance to set up another prospect is never higher than on your next call. Double down and keep dialing.

Know Your Numbers

How will you mentally deal with the unavoidable hang-ups and the deflating "I am not interested!" and "Call me in six months!" responses from a prospect, though? How will you react if for weeks you simply cannot get through to the decision maker at what you deem to be a great prospect? First of all, don't take it personally. People are not rejecting you personally when they refuse to engage on a call. They are just rejecting the offer you are making them.

A 100 percent success rate doesn't exist, and it certainly doesn't exist in sales. For sales champions that's absolutely okay. It's acceptable because they know their numbers and how many calls they have to make on average to set up a meeting.

Reggie Jackson struck out 2,597 times and had a .262 batting average, "failing" three out of four times on average. Yet he is one of the most successful players who ever stepped up to the plate, being inducted into the National Baseball Hall of Fame in 1993. You have to look at cold calling the same way. On average, every "no" gets you closer to the next "yes." And while this is certainly one of the oldest sales clichés, it is also still true.

OUTREACH SYSTEM

Plan your outreach work and then work the plan. It starts with determining one of the most important metrics in new business sales: the number of first-time, face-to-face meetings you are planning to set up with new prospects every week. What that number is, of course, depends on your industry and market as well as your product and service. Even within the same sales team these numbers will vary by salesperson, as many factors play into them (length of existing account list, focus categories, etc.). This weekly goal should be put in writing and come from you, with coaching input from your manager. You are the one who needs to buy into it and be in charge of exceeding it—week after week. Track this number, even throughout the week. If you are pacing behind by Wednesday, increase your outreach time, for example with additional cold-calling hours on Thursday and Friday.

There is a direct correlation between this metric and your new business success in the future. But in order to manage your business effectively, it needs to be accurate. If you feed your CRM system with new business meetings that were never really confirmed, or were kept purposefully vague from the prospects' side, only to get your manager off your back, you are not doing yourself a favor. It's amazing how quickly a "call me back later in the week" in a prospect's email reply can turn into "Strategic Discovery Meeting Thursday 3 PM" in your CRM. By doing this, you are also reducing the accuracy of your individual conversion and closing ratios. This all results in you not being able to play the "numbers game" as discussed earlier.

There Is Never a Perfect Time

"When is the best time to make a cold call?"
"Are cold calls more effective in the morning or in the afternoon?"
"Is early in the week or Friday better for a walk-in to an office?"
"When are prospects more likely to open my emails and read them?"

The amount of advice on these topics—in articles, books, or You-Tube videos—is astounding. With a couple of exceptions we will get to, it's also mostly irrelevant. The best time to reach out is . . . *RIGHT* . . . *NOW!* Cold-call reluctance is one of the biggest issues affecting the average new business salesperson. There is always a "better time" to call for them, often not much more than a made-up excuse not to pick up the phone this second.

Of course, there are certain tactics that will improve your conversion ratio. For example, it absolutely does make sense to switch up the time of your daily cold-calling hours. Calling at a different hour every morning will increase your chance to actually connect with a prospect. It also makes sense to call hard-to-reach prospects during the five-minute span before the top or the bottom of the hour. Executives typically start meetings or conference calls at :00 or :30 of the hour, and the likelihood they will be at their desk or at least not busy in another meeting is potentially a little higher during these moments. This all makes logical sense. But overall, "timing" a call is a losing strategy. Salespeople who cold-call daily and consistently will always be more successful than those who are waiting for the perfect moment to connect.

Develop a Cold-Calling Routine

Your cold-calling success will increase by developing certain routines. For starters, set up cold-calling hours in your Outlook calendar as noncancelable appointments with yourself, and then stick to them. I know how tempting it is to skip a calling session to instead write a proposal, attend a brainstorm meeting, or put out a fire with your most important client. Don't do it. A typical cold-calling session in a B2B scenario lasts about forty-five minutes to an hour. If you schedule two of these daily—one in the morning, one in the afternoon—you will have more than enough time to get all the other, most likely more enjoyable work done. And even your most important client will understand and be willing to wait for sixty minutes to get a call back from you.

If you need some inspiration to form your routine, look no further than Arnold Schwarzenegger. You can find several interviews and speeches online in which he takes on the topic, using examples from his bodybuilding and acting days to make his point. Here are a few of Arnold's tips that are particularly relevant to cold calling:

- Make it a daily activity, so it becomes a habit you don't even have to think about, so that it almost starts automatically. It is actually easier to work out six times a week instead of once or twice a week. Likewise, it's actually easier to cold-call if you do it daily.
- Break up the routine into several manageable chunks of shorter duration. Two shorter cold-calling sessions a day make more sense than one longer session. Forty-five focused minutes twice a day should do it in most industries.
- Win the morning! Schwarzenegger talks a lot about doing full-fledged squats with 500 pounds at 5:30 AM when he was getting ready to compete in the Mr. Universe contest. While you don't have to go to that kind of extreme, starting to call early is important. Shut off your email, review who you are planning to call, and start dialing. Warm up by calling a few friendly customers first, then keep the momentum going. Nothing will have a bigger impact on having a successful day than a fruitful cold-calling session in the morning. So don't push it off. Once you start procrastinating, you will never catch up. As your day progresses, unexpected things will get in your way, and before you know it the day is over. Early morning calls work. You have a higher chance of reaching key executives before 8 AM than after. Calling people early also conveys to them that you are a self-motivated person they can count on once they are doing business with you.
- Go for *ONE MORE*! It doesn't matter if it's one more bench press or one more cold call. Your results will improve, especially if you look at it over time. One cold call more per cold-calling session adds up to around 500 additional cold calls per year. I have heard of some successful salespeople following the mantra of "8 before

8 and 5 after 5": they make eight additional cold calls before 8 AM, and five cold calls after 5 PM. How can that not get you results?

Welcome to Heavy Metal Sales

In a business environment where decision makers are bombarded by hundreds of messages per week, it is not easy to stand out. It will not be uncommon at all for your first couple of messages (voicemail, email, or whatever other tactic you are using) to be completely missed by the prospect. As a result, you need to get used to being persistent.

Unfortunately, less experienced salespeople are often hesitant to reach out to a prospect too often, as if the person on the other end is sitting there keeping count of the number of outreach efforts, determining that "this guy is a pest." As a result, they let way too much time go by between calls or emails and never make an impact. Sales outreach is not about being pushy, it's about being professionally persistent. Look at your attempts to connect with a new prospect as the equivalent of a full-blown marketing campaign that uses several different tactics over a short period.

Several years ago, Juergen Klopp—at the time of writing, manager of the Liverpool British Premier League football (or soccer) club—coined the term "Heavy Metal Football." It describes a type of play characterized by high pressing, quick passing, and a very hard work rate. It is an in-your-face style of football: fast, aggressive, and exciting. When executing your marketing campaign to score the meeting with your prospect, you will need a similar mindset, a "Heavy Metal Sales" mindset: full pressure, many touchpoints, and a high level of perseverance.

Heavy Metal Sales means creating ten touchpoints in ten (work)days.

Rookie salesperson: *"I am not sure I can think of ten ways to get in touch with a prospect."*

It's actually not that hard. But it's work. You can, for example, send an introductory email (a.k.a. a seed email), connect on LinkedIn, leave a voicemail teasing an idea, send a case study by email or by snail mail, send a LinkedIn message with a new insight, leave another voicemail with a different reason to meet with you, send a handwritten note, do an in-person

Figure 7.1: Example for Heavy Metal Sales Approach

walk-in to the prospect's office, and many, many other things (we will get to some creative examples to set up meetings in chapter eleven).

Rookie salesperson: *"Won't people get annoyed?"*

Not if you switch up your message. There is power in making your attempts over a very short time. But be smart about it and mix it up. Of course, you don't want to leave two voicemails per day for a week. That would be considered stalking. But be persistent. You would be surprised how often prospects apologized to me for not returning my voicemail or not replying to my emails, when I eventually got them on the phone or met them in person. You might think you are annoying them with your outreach attempts, but most of the time your attempts don't even register with them.

Your cold-calling attempts run parallel to these ten touchpoints, as shown in Figure 7.1. If you have developed the routine of scheduling (and keeping) two cold-calling sessions per day, or ten a week, that means you are adding another twenty opportunities to connect with your prospect live over the course of two workweeks. We will discuss how to do that in chapter eight.

The Heavy Metal Sales approach is even more important if the brand awareness of your company or your company's product is not very high. You first might have to increase the prospect's familiarity with you and your company before the prospect will engage with you.

In sales, consistently relying on one tactic or method (usually the one where the salesperson expects the least amount of resistance and rejection, which these days mostly means relying only on email or social media) will generate mediocre results at best. I have seen people conduct these Heavy Metal Sales campaigns with several people at the same company—at the same time, not in the form of mass emails, but with an individualized approach. Of course, that is even more work, but for your dream leads, absolutely worth it.

Tips for Focused Cold Calling

Most salespeople are more effective and efficient if they group their calls by segment, making calls to prospects in one industry first, followed by calls to prospects in another industry. That helps because similar companies usually share a comparable set of issues and challenges, and you can use many of the same RBRs and case studies, saving you time. Here are several other tips to keep you focused during your cold-calling sessions:

- Find a quiet place without interruptions instead of calling from your office desk. Many salespeople are actually hesitant to make cold calls while their office neighbors could potentially be listening. Don't feel bad about it for a second. The best salespeople I have worked with don't make their cold calls at their desk. Your productivity will be much higher in a conference room or a cold-calling pod. With laptops or iPads or working remotely that's very easy to do.

- You are only doing one thing during a cold-calling session, and that is cold calling. This is not the time to send seed emails or LinkedIn messages. Your email alerts should be off so you don't get tempted to open one every five minutes. Your cell phone should be silenced and ideally out of sight. This is not the time to multitask.
- Complete your research before you start calling. Then all you need to do is pull up the information about your prospect in Salesforce, get the phone number, and start dialing.
- Keep track of what type of RBR you were using when you reached out. Ideally, you captured this in your CRM system, so you can easily go back and look before you reach out the next time with a different RBR, or before you actually meet the prospect for the first time. You need to know what hook got you in the door.
- Capture all information you receive on these calls, such as the name of the gatekeeper. I have found that salespeople make these notes more efficiently by hand. Then, once they are done with the cold-calling session, they enter them into their CRMs.

YOUR RELEVANT BUSINESS REASON

To become successful in setting up face-to-face meetings with new business prospects, you need to master the art of crafting an effective RBR—the core element of your cold-calling script as well as the seed email and LinkedIn messages we will create in the next chapters. While we were focused on the *how* and *how often* on the previous pages, an RBR is all about *what* you will be saying or writing. Even the best and most customized RBR doesn't guarantee you a meeting—but it does improve your odds. And that's what sales is all about: doing all the little things right throughout the entire sales process to maximize your chances of making a sale.

Think of the RBR as the *key talking point* you will be using when connecting with the prospect—the reason most relevant to the prospect, not you. Or as Mike Weinberg describes it in his excellent book *New Sales. Simplified*, it's a "delicious, mouth-watering tease that creates a strong hunger for the main course, which is the face-to-face meeting we are pursuing."

Short, Concise, and Compelling

One of the cardinal rules at the start: your RBR needs to be short, concise, and compelling. And while you might think this is logical—after all, you are interrupting your prospect's day—you would be surprised how often this rule is broken, not just by new salespeople but also by more experienced sellers. It sometimes seems that because they have more knowledge about the details of their product or service, they want to cram too much into one RBR. As a result, you see cold-call scripts that take thirty seconds to make a point or seed emails that are so long the person on the receiving end needs to do as much scrolling as reading. When reaching out to prospects, you win in the first ten seconds or you lose. In person it might even be less time than that because of how quickly the brain reacts. You have very little room for error, and once you stumble at the beginning it's very hard to recover.

The RBR shouldn't really change much based on the outreach channel you are using (phone, email, in-person, etc.). Yes, the message will change as part of the cadence of our Heavy Metal outreach campaign, and, as a result, the prospect will receive different RBRs over the course of ten days. But don't throw your best RBRs out the window only because you are using a different channel. I have seen too many salespeople develop a very solid RBR for a cold call over the phone, only to completely abandon it when they stopped in at the prospect's office. Suddenly, the effective RBR morphed into *"Do you have ten minutes for me?"*—making them sound like every other salesperson.

There Are Four Effective Relevant Business Reasons . . .

Four different categories account for 99 percent of effective RBRs, as shown in Figure 7.2.

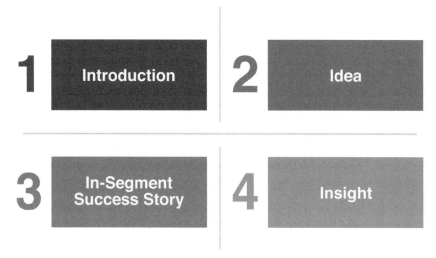

Figure 7.2: Four Different Relevant Business Reasons

Your success rate in getting a prospect to meet with you will increase dramatically if you can identify someone in your network who is connected to your prospect and is willing to make an **INTRODUCTION** for you. You can do this by email or maybe even in person over lunch or dinner. Even if your network ultimately does not make a direct introduction, using the mutual acquaintance's name in your outreach as part of the RBR is also very effective. That's why it always makes sense to check LinkedIn and see if you and your prospect have a mutual connection. While introductions and referrals will probably make up the minority of your RBRs, they are exactly the ones that sales champions explore first.

New **IDEAS** and new concepts are a very effective method of attracting the interest of a prospect. Maybe it is a promotional idea you came up with to help your prospect during a new product launch. Maybe it is a more process-driven innovation that can help your prospect reduce the production cycle by 40 percent. Maybe it is a concept for a sponsorship of an event your company is producing that targets an audience the prospect covets. Be careful, though: don't give away too much initially. If you flesh out the entire idea or concept on your cold call, your prospect might not see the need to meet with you in person. When you lead with ideas, it's also important to try to create some type of urgency, by highlighting limited availability and exclusivity. For Idea RBRs, I like to use the first word or phrases *"Imagine...,"* *"What if...,"* *"Picture this...,"* or *"Right now..."*

Using an **IN-SEGMENT SUCCESS STORY** in your outreach is a very effective method to stand out from the sales pack. Prospects want to know what is working for other companies in their industry or territory. They want to find out if they have been missing out on things by not partnering with your company earlier. They might even think they can gain some knowledge from you about what their competitors are doing. One specific success story with clear results will be more effective here than just saying "We have a proven track record with other companies in your industry."

An **INSIGHT** is a piece of relevant information that the prospect will most likely—to the best of your knowledge—not be aware of and will find intriguing and interesting. It could be a research fact about consumer behavior or a statistic or trend that influences an entire industry. Many times, to make the insight more believable, it involves an actual number or percentage. It's also important to understand what an insight is *not*: it is *not* a fact about your company! Insights are effective because they immediately increase your competence level in the eyes of the prospect, which helps you reduce resistance by making prospects feel you could be a resource they are able to count on.

You should always strive to have at least a couple of RBRs ready for each prospect. Sometimes, if you run into a lot of resistance and have to battle several objections, you will be forced to use up all your RBRs on the first phone call. Other times you will use them in your follow-up attempts on other channels in order to find different angles that might pique the prospect's interest.

... and Many Bad Ones

Notice what did *not* make the list of potential RBRs:

- Leading with the fact that your company is *"number one,"* *"the best,"* *"the biggest,"* *"the cheapest"* or any other superlative about you or the company you represent.

- RBRs that offer nothing more than wasting the prospect's time, like *"I would love to stop by to tell you more about our company"* or *"I would love to set up a meeting to find out more about your business and your needs."*
- Something everyone already knows, dressed up as an insight. *"During the coronavirus pandemic, homeschooling is expected to increase"* comes to mind. Duh!
- A list of features, figures, and facts no one cares about.
- Something sneaky that might get you in the door, but will backfire later. In the radio and TV business, that could be the old *"We would love to have you as a guest on the show,"* when what the salesperson really wants to meet about is how to sell an advertising campaign for money. Never hide the fact that your goal is to get the prospect as a customer.
- A detailed description of the solution you are offering. Less experienced salespeople make this mistake all the time. Remember: the goal is to sell them on meeting face to face with you, not to sell them on the solution, at least not yet. What's in it for them, their benefit, is more important than explaining *how* your offering works.
- Openings like *"I am following up on my email"* or *"Did you get the email I sent you?"* Both make it much too easy for the prospect to end a call quickly: *"I didn't get it. Can you please resend it. Thanks and goodbye."* Ouch! This response is very hard to recover from, so why put yourself in this position in the first place? If you did send a prior email, just treat the cold call as if you are reaching out for the first time. If prospects remember your email, they will most likely mention it. *"Didn't you send me an email?"* With a quick *"Yes, what did you think about it?"* you are in the middle of a conversation that you can then steer toward additional RBRs.
- In the media world, statements like *"I saw your ad in . . ."* or *"I heard your commercial on . . ."* at the beginning of a call or email are probably some of the most overused and least effective RBRs you can choose. How are these in any shape or form relevant for or compelling to the prospect?

Avoid "Salesy" Language

Your goal in sales is always to be perceived as a businessperson, not as a salesperson a couple rungs down the ladder. Busy prospects want to deal with peers, not salespeople who sound like they are selling something. Many phrases and words can paint you into that sales corner quickly and have no place in an RBR:

- *"It's an honor speaking with you."*
- *"We are proud to . . ."*
- Words and phrases like *"unique," "one-of-a-kind," "state-of-the-art," "groundbreaking," "world-class," "best-in-class," "amazing," "game changer," "innovative solution,"* etc.

There are many more words and phrases like this, but you get the idea. They are not only way too overused for you to stand out, they are also mostly an exaggeration and irrelevant. You would never use them in real life when talking to a friend ("Let's watch this one-of-a-kind movie!"), so why would you use them here?

There is also a special place in sales hell for salespeople who add the word "just" to pretty much everything they are asking or saying. "Just" could be one of the worst words to use when you want to make an impression, not only in sales, in many areas of life. *"I just want to take you out for dinner"* when trying to ask out a woman doesn't sound as confident as *"Let's have dinner."* Likewise, sentences like *"I'm just calling to find out if you are interested in seeing a proposal", "This is just a . . .", "I am just checking in . . .", "I am just following up . . ."*, and other *"I am just . . ."* sentences don't do much more than tempt the prospect to press the delete button or get off the phone quickly.

On the other hand, words like *"accelerate," "amplify," "strengthen," "maximize," "improve," "imagine," "share," "save," "grow,"* or *"partner,"* just to give a few examples, are much stronger and convey your desired image as a businessperson and not a salesperson more effectively.

Take the Prospect's Background into Account

Always craft your RBR with an eye on the buyers' backgrounds, experience, and current positions and roles. What do you think are their priorities? What will get their attention? What could be their current concerns and potential objections? These days, you can find most information on background and expertise on LinkedIn, and some online tools like Winmo even offer potentially helpful personality insights on many buyers.

As an example, if your LinkedIn search determines your general manager prospect is a CPA and came up the finance route, and Winmo is telling you this particular executive is "analytical, pragmatic, skeptical, and collected," your best RBR is probably not a very creative, outrageous, right-brain idea. Instead, you might be better off leading with a case study or insight that includes hard data on items like ROI, expense savings, or margins.

CASE STUDY: RELEVANT BUSINESS REASONS FOR REBECCA GYMS

You check LinkedIn for any mutual connections with Tracy Ranner, the chief marketing officer, and come up short. You decide to call Rob Meyers, an old acquaintance of yours, who runs an advertising agency in Los Angeles, and ask him if he knows Tracy or anyone else at Rebecca Gyms. It turns out that he had worked with Tracy on a couple of projects in her old job. He gives you permission to use his name in your outreach. In addition, you craft one RBR for each of the other RBR areas—Idea, Insight, In-Segment Success Story—that we are planning to use during our Heavy Metal outreach strategy, shown in Figure 7.3.

1

Introduction
"Rob Meyers suggested we should connect on your planned New York expansion. The two of us worked together on several marketing projects in the Northeast."

2

Idea
"Imagine if we create a movement of New York women who hold each other accountable to work out on a regular basis. A movement that is led by our female radio personalities."

3

In-Segment Success Story
"We recently helped Y7 Studio launch their new brand as well as ten new locations here in New York, and as a result they surpassed their initial membership goals by 43%."

4

Insight
"67 % of New York women between the ages of 25 and 49 don't belong to a gym. That is a pool of 1.1 million potential members of Rebecca Gyms."

Figure 7.3: Four Effective Relevant Business Reasons for Rebecca Gyms

8

THE MOMENT OF TRUTH

Effective Relevant Business Reasons will work for all outreach channels. In this chapter, as well as chapters nine, ten, and eleven, we will incorporate them into broader messages we will use to connect with prospects by phone, in writing, and in person.

Of all the sales tools available, the phone is still the most powerful. Many salespeople, especially younger ones, will try to debate this.

"Nobody picks up the phone anymore."

"Sending emails is so much more efficient."

"It's not like it used to be. People get irritated when I call them."

I hear these statements often, usually from people who are not hitting their numbers. But I firmly believe the most successful salespeople know how to use the phone to set up face-to-face meetings with decision makers.

I don't even agree with the argument that cold calling has gotten harder over the last few years. It's always been hard. It's always been the least favorite part of everyone's job. When underperforming salespeople argue it is no longer effective, it always seems as if they are actually hoping they are right, so they can finally give up on cold calling for good and focus instead on blasting out one email after another or posting and sharing articles on LinkedIn. Rejection is so much easier to take that way, right? A hang up or a "not interested" over the phone is worse for the ego than no reply to an email.

YOUR FRIEND—THE PHONE

Contact and conversion rates are higher with outreach over the phone. In many industries, contact rates have actually been rising over the last decade. It's hard to say exactly why prospects are answering their phones more often, but it could have something to do with the fact that many decision makers no longer have secretaries or assistants, who used to shield them from sales calls. Instead, many have their office calls forwarded to their cell phones, or their cell is their only phone line. That means that they no longer have to physically be at their desks for you to reach them. It is true, though, that their phones are just not ringing as often as in the past. With most salespeople choosing the easy route of email, decision makers' email in-boxes are flooded with hundreds of sales offers, while their phones stay silent. Sales champions see this as a great opportunity. Approaching a prospect by phone is actually helping you differentiate yourself from other salespeople more than ever.

It is also much easier nowadays to find phone numbers of companies and decision makers online. Sources range from the company's website (usually in the About the Company or Contact Us sections) to online sales platforms like Owler, RocketReach, Winmo, or Hunter.

If for some reason you are not able to find the names of potential decision makers during your prospecting research, pick up the phone, call the company, and ask. *"I need your help. Who decides on . . . ?"* is usually a good way to start. If you can't get anywhere through the usual departments, try the sales department. The typical salesperson will empathize with you and try to help you out with a name and potentially even extension and email address.

SCRIPTS AND TALKING POINTS

Your RBR constitutes the core of your phone message. If you are new to sales entirely or in a new sales role at a new company, write down the entire script, word by word. I know what you are thinking: scripts sound rehearsed, they make you sound canned, and are usually too long. That is true—to some degree. In the wrong hands, scripts can actually make your call less effective. The last thing the person on the other end of the line needs is someone interrupting their day with a message that sounds like it is read from a teleprompter. However, writing a script does force you to think through your phone message in its entirety, from beginning to end, in a logically structured way. Actors also work off scripts and don't actually sound scripted. That's your goal here, too.

The more experienced you become in your new sales role, the less you will have to rely on entire scripts. Instead, you will focus more on talking points that outline your call. Write these talking points down so you're better prepared and to make your calls sound more consistent. You want to use the most compelling statements over and over, instead of constantly making up new lines on the fly.

START STRONG

When you outline your message, one rule stands above all others: the first ten seconds count! Similar to a TV or radio commercial that has to engage you right from the beginning to earn the right to your attention for the rest of the ad, you have to make an impact from the moment your prospect picks up the phone. Different studies have shown that prospects will have made up their minds after ten seconds. Ten seconds *max*, that is! During those ten seconds you have to convey to prospects that you are an expert on what you are calling about *and* that you are someone worth listening to further. That's not easy, which is why your message has to be concise and engaging off the bat. As mentioned earlier, your tonality, confidence, and energy level will play a big part in creating this immediate impression as well.

EFFECTIVE COLD-CALL FRAMEWORK

Let's break down the entire phone message into seven components, structured around the chosen RBR. The resulting cold-calling framework is
shown in Figure 8.1.

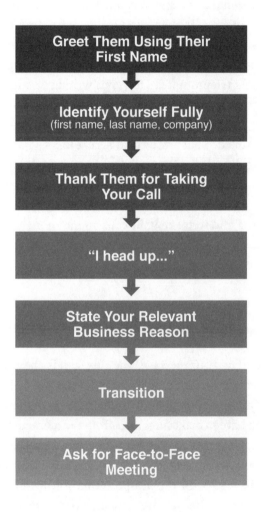

Figure 8.1: Effective Cold-Call Framework

Let's take a closer look at each of these seven components.

Greeting

Begin the call with a confident "Good morning" or "Hi" followed by the prospect's first name. It seems trivial, but people everywhere, in all positions, industries, and countries, like hearing their names. In the United States, it has become absolutely acceptable to use someone's first name, even if you have never met the person before. That's not the case everywhere, by the way. In languages like French, Spanish, or German, salespeople have to actively decide which pronoun to use ("tu" or "vous" in French, "tu" or "usted" in Spanish, "Du" or "Sie" in German), since these are signifying informal or formal ways to address a person. You don't have to worry about that when you are selling in English and in the US. There's no need to address a prospect with "Mr." or "Ms.," either, maybe with the exception of the medical field, when you'd probably say "Doctor," followed by the person's last name. But in general, *"Good morning, Tracy"* will do.

Identification

Use your first and last name, followed by the name of your company. You don't need to mention your title, position, or role. We'll get to that. I never understood why some salespeople are hesitant to give their name or their company's name at the beginning of a cold call. Avoiding a confident identification is an approach that almost always backfires. While you are going over the RBR, all the prospect is thinking is *"Who is this guy?"* It's just not an effective technique. People like transparency, and—unless you are selling something illegal—there is absolutely no reason not to give your full name and the name of your company at the start of the call. It demonstrates that you are a professional, a businessperson.

"Thanks for taking my call"

Yes, thanking the prospect for picking up the phone will take up a second or two. But, trust me, it's time well spent, because at this point of the call, the prospect's defense shield is at its strongest:

"Do I know this person?"

"Is this a sales call?"

"Should I come up with an excuse and get off the phone right now?"

"Damn, I wish I hadn't picked up!"

Thanking the prospect for taking the call lowers the prospect's resistance level because you're acknowledging that you are intruding on their day. Sometimes, prospects will respond affirmatively at that moment of the call (*"Sure"*); other times, they won't say anything. In both cases, you just bought additional time to build up your authority with your follow-up statement. Thanking them for taking the call is also much more effective than asking *"How are you?"*

"I head up . . ."

I have been using the line *"I head up . . ."* for many years and it has always served me well. Seeing it suggested in several courses and books on cold calling over the last few years has reinforced my belief that, as simple as these three words sound, they are true difference makers. They make you stand out from other salespeople by enhancing your position and elevating your authority level in the prospect's mind: *"Maybe I should pay attention to this person."*

But the phrase *"I head up"* does even more than that. It also increases your own self-confidence. No one wants to sound like a salesperson or—even worse—telemarketer, and stating, *"I head up"* makes you feel like an executive who is in charge of something.

The truth is, even if your business card might not convey it, we all are in charge of something:

"I head up event sponsorships."

"I head up the Healthcare vertical."

"I head up shopper marketing partnerships."

You just need to determine what makes the most sense for your role. You should also feel free to change up what you are "heading up" depending on which prospect you are calling. Don't use your job title here. Everyone does that. Use whatever makes you look like a true expert in whatever field you think the prospect is most interested.

Give Your Relevant Business Reason

It's "go" time. The prospect knows who you are, where you are calling from, and what you do. Now it's time to tell your prospect why you are calling. You already did the heavy lifting here by thinking of an RBR in advance: an idea, an insight, or an In-Segment Success Story. If you can drop the name of a referral, even better. Just proceed in a quick and concise manner. Your prospect won't be willing to sit through a twenty-second RBR.

Transition to What's Next

Before we can ask for the face-to-face meeting, we need to explain why such a meeting would be beneficial to the prospect. Such a transitional statement builds on the RBR and paints the picture of what the prospect can expect in the actual meeting. It also reduces the stress level on the prospect's side when you're transparent about your intentions. People are more comfortable when they know what to expect:

"I think the best place to start would be for me to show you some initial ideas . . ."

"I'd love to come in and walk you through the detailed case study . . ."

"Let's get together to see if we are a fit . . ."

"From there we can decide if it makes sense to have a deeper conversation . . ."

With statements like these, you are setting up the actual ask for the meeting perfectly.

Ask for the Face-To-Face Meeting

Get straight to the point and forcefully ask for the meeting. Be confident and direct:

"Does next Monday early afternoon work for a video call?"

"How about we meet next Wednesday at 2 PM?"

"I can stop by your office next Tuesday at 10 AM."

Give the time as specifically as possible—don't just offer "to meet next week." Then shut up. Give your prospect time to respond. It takes a moment to process all the information you just went through on the call.

Most likely, the prospect will not grant your request. That's right. Even after calling fully prepared and full of energy and confidence, with a strong, prospect-focused RBR, voiced in the right tone, chances are the prospect will say no to you. Buyers are simply receiving too many messages from salespeople throughout the day. Their automatic reaction is set to *"no meeting."* Don't take it personally. It's not you; it's a fact of sales life. Expecting the objection is already half the battle, and we will cover how to respond in chapter twelve.

Still, be prepared to ask for the meeting three times. Remember, we look at this part of the sales process as Heavy Metal Sales. This is the time to put the pedal to the metal and to push past resistance if needed. Fight for the meeting. Often that means using up additional RBRs to convince the prospect to invest precious face-to-face time with you. That's why you always want to have more than one RBR at your fingertips.

One last tip for scheduling the meeting: portray yourself as a business-person whose time is as valuable as your prospect's. Offering up meetings for the following day or statements like *"I am very flexible time-wise"* or *"I have the entire day open, what works best for you?"* are detrimental to that goal. You want prospects to believe you are working with many different accounts that need to be serviced.

The length of the meeting you are requesting depends on your industry and what you are planning to cover with the prospect. I've found that asking for forty-five-minute discovery meetings has worked well for me over the years. If the meeting runs long for whatever reason, it's unlikely the prospect would have scheduled another meeting at :45 (or :15) of the hour, and I can still cover everything needed. At the same time, a thirty-minute meeting wouldn't allow for more detailed discussions and for agreeing on a clear follow-up assignment, which is the goal of the first meeting.

CASE STUDY: COLD-CALL SCRIPT FOR REBECCA GYMS

Based on the RBRs we developed for Rebecca Gyms in the previous chapter, one way to approach CMO Tracy Ranner is to use our In-Segment Success Story RBR in our cold call. Here is the message broken down into its seven components:

Step 1—Greeting:
"Good morning, Tracy."

Step 2—Identification:
"This is Dave Gahan with NYC Media in New York."

Step 3:
"Thanks for taking my call."

Step 4:
"I head up the Health and Fitness vertical here."

Step 5—RBR:
"Tracy, we recently helped Y7 Studio launch ten new locations in New York. And as a result, they surpassed their membership goals by 43 percent."

Step 6—Transition:
"I'd love to schedule a meeting to share with you what exactly worked for them and go over some potential learnings for your upcoming launch in New York. From there we can decide if it makes sense to have a deeper conversation."

Step 7—Ask:

"Since you are based in San Diego, does next Monday early afternoon work for a forty-five-minute video call? Maybe 2 PM?"

The cold-call script would therefore look like this:

"Good morning, Tracy. This is Dave Gahan with NYC Media in New York. Thanks for taking my call. I head up the Health and Fitness vertical here. Tracy, we recently helped Y7 Studio launch ten new locations in New York. And as a result, they surpassed their membership goals by 43 percent. I'd love to schedule a meeting to share with you what exactly worked for them and go over some potential learnings for your upcoming launch in New York. From there we can decide if it makes sense to have a deeper conversation. Since you are based in San Diego, does next Monday early afternoon work for a forty-five-minute video call? Maybe 2 PM?"

Here is another cold-call script for Rebecca Gyms, this time using the "Idea" RBR you developed:

"Good morning, Tracy. This is Dave Gahan at NYC Media in New York. Thanks for taking my call. I head up the Health and Fitness vertical here and heard about your plans to launch Rebecca Gyms in New York. Tracy, imagine if we create a movement of New York women, led by our female radio personalities and bloggers, that hold each other accountable to work out on a regular basis. I think that would make an impact quickly and drive new memberships. I wanted to schedule some time and flesh this out a little bit more with you. From there we can decide if it makes sense to have a deeper conversation. Does Monday early afternoon work for a forty-five-minute video call? Maybe 2 PM?"

9

MAXIMIZING EMAIL CONVERSION RATES

S eed emails to new business prospects, sometimes also referred to as "cold email marketing," are important tools in strategic and comprehensive Heavy Metal outreach campaigns. They can certainly be a very effective and efficient way to set up face-to-face meetings with prospects. But using *only* seed emails, and forgetting about all the other tools available, is a sure way to mediocrity. In addition, ineffective email campaigns don't just make you look like an amateur; they can also quickly annoy the prospect and block your access for a long time, if not forever.

The fact that prospects don't just receive emails from B2B salespeople, but also from consumer-focused companies who might have gotten access or even bought their email addresses, limits the effectiveness of seed emails tremendously. You are not just competing with your competitors for share of voice of email in-boxes, you are competing with everyone. Add to that the fact that most emails are opened on smartphones and not computers, with personal and business emails all blending together in one email in-box, and you start to realize what you are up against. Most emails we receive have no relevance to us and are terribly written. They look like spam and most likely are. No wonder open rates have dropped dramatically over the past decade.

LEARN FROM THE PROS

What I wish I could show you is some type of magic silver bullet in the form of a seed email to secure a meeting with a prospect. Unfortunately, that simply does not exist in sales. There are just too many factors that play into this. The actual content of your email is just one of them.

You can literally send the worst seed email that was ever sent in the history of sales and score a meeting if, for example, the prospect was just told by her manager that—for budgeting and accounting reasons—she needs to spend $200,000 by the end of June or lose the money to a different department. You will get the meeting. I can guarantee it. You will get it even if your seed email didn't follow any of the rules and tips you will be learning over the next few pages. On the other hand, you can write your best email ever, but if the person you sent it to split up with his girlfriend the night before, he might not want to engage with anyone or anything right now. Every sales situation is unique, and timing and even luck play a big role.

What we can do, though, is improve our odds by using tactics that have been tested. The good thing about seed emails is that there is a lot of data available on what works well and what works less well, usually based on testing of different email campaigns by B2C marketers. We can use their learnings to make our seed emails more effective as a result. Replacing a word here, using a different Relevant Business Reason or subject line there—that's how we maximize our chances of getting a positive response.

For you to see success in using seed emails to set up face-to-face meetings with new business prospects, your email needs to do three things: it needs to reach the right person, that person needs to open the email, and—once they open it— the body of your email needs to convince them to agree to the meeting.

REACHING THE RIGHT PERSON

Similar to finding a prospect's phone number, tracking down the email address of a prospect has become easier over the years. Many companies list the email addresses of executives on their website. New online tools that allow you to search for email addresses, like hunter.io, are regularly launched. If all else fails, you can always call the company and ask someone for the prospect's email address. People are usually less hesitant giving out email information than phone extensions. If you are hitting a wall with all of these tactics, try to find out the format of a company's email addresses and give it your best shot.

What you want to avoid at all costs is sending seed emails to generic email addresses like support@company.com or info@company.com, because these emails won't land in the in-box of any potential influencer, let alone a senior decision maker, and you won't receive any meaningful response. It is a true waste of your valuable sales time. Instead, use some of this time for further research. There are very few instances where it will not be possible to find any contact information.

For your emails to be seen by prospects, they need to make it into their email in-boxes. This is by no means guaranteed, as many companies today have spam filters set up that either block emails entirely or automatically move them into junk folders. Research from 2019 shows that email has an in-box placement rate of about 85 percent. That's pretty good, but also means that close to one out of every six emails are either blocked or filtered to spam. Don't take that risk. Spam filtering has become more rigorous over the past few years, a trend that likely will continue. And since a B2B seed email is—by definition—one that the receiver has not opted in to, you certainly want to at least be aware what constitutes spam and what does not.

Spam filters check for red flags in both the subject line and the body of the email, like:

- Embedded hyperlinks
- Messages in ALL CAPS
- Colorful and different-sized fonts
- Attachments: There are other reasons why it doesn't make sense to include attachments in a seed email, but if you need one more, the fact that using them increases the risk of having your email sent to a junk folder should probably do.
- Bulk emails: Seed emails should be sent to one individual, one email at a time.
- Too many unopened emails sent to the same person in a short period of time: That's one of the reasons you should limit the number of emails sent to the same prospect during a typical two-week Heavy Metal outreach campaign to three.

Spam filters try to catch suspicious phrases and words associated with scams, gimmicks, schemes, promises, or free gifts. As the saying goes, *"if it sounds too good to be true, it probably is."* And while the list of spam-risky phrases constantly changes, here is a short selection:

- Increase sales
- Increase traffic
- Amazing
- Once-in-a-lifetime
- Incredible deal
- Special promotion
- Great offer
- Opportunity
- Congratulations
- Guarantee

Sales champions don't have to worry about this. They wouldn't use most of these words in the first place, not because they could be considered spam, but because they just sound way too "salesy" to be effective. They are bad salesmanship.

Your email provider may have a built-in tool that checks your emails for spam trigger words before sending it. Alternatively, you can also use ISnotSPAM, a free online tool that scores your email for deliverability and checks if it is likely to trigger spam filters.

THE SUBJECT LINE: THE EMAIL EQUIVALENT OF A NEWSPAPER HEADLINE

For more than three centuries, newspaper headlines have served one primary function: to pique the interest of the reader enough to read the actual article, or—in the case of the front-page headline—to buy the paper. A good email subject line does something very similar. It gets the prospect to open the email and read the actual message. If your subject line (and your opening sentence; more on that shortly) isn't enticing, it doesn't matter how great the content of your email is. No one will ever see it. At a time when most people are checking in-boxes on their smartphones (in many cases even when they are sitting in front of their computers because it's just faster and more convenient), your beautifully crafted email is one swipe to the right away from oblivion.

Much of the advice covered in the chapter on RBRs also applies to subject lines, and maybe even more so. For example, focusing on your own product or company will lower opening rates dramatically.

Based on a 2018 study by Yesware, the following subject line tactics were proven to be the most effective in maximizing email opening rates:

- Keep the subject line to thirty characters or less. The research showed a clear negative correlation between length of subject line and opening rate.
- Personalize the subject line as much as possible. If you can, reference a recent accomplishment (*"Loved your article in Fortune"*) or a common contact (*"John Perry suggested I reach out"*).
- If nothing else, try to incorporate the name of the company you are reaching out to into the subject line. People love seeing

the brand name with which they are associated. It will increase opening rates. Example: *"Elvis Duran loves Nutella."*

- Generic, impersonal, and boring subject lines won't help you break through the clutter. Instead, create curiosity and urgency.
- Stay away from questions in the subject line, such as *"Can you chat?"* Too many consumer-facing companies have been using questions, which has lowered their effectiveness over time. You also sound too much like a salesperson.
- Along those lines, "salesy" language like the terms just covered (*"one-of-a-kind," "unique,"* etc.) significantly lowered opening rates as well.

One very successful subject line tactic is to tie it to an actual RBR, but as an even shorter statement in the form of a headline. For example, if your RBR is based on a success story, a possible subject line could be *"2 tactics that worked for XYZ."* If the RBR is based on an insight that includes a number or statistic, your subject line could be *"Only 19% of NYC restaurant launches succeed."* If the RBR is based on an idea, you can tease it in the subject line as well.

The reality is, though, there is no secret formula for creating the perfect email subject line every single time. What works in one industry might not work in another. What works in one situation might not be right in another. What applies to everyone is that you have to follow the law. A subject line like *"Thanks for your order"* would most likely be effective—after all, a prospect who has never heard of you would probably open it to find out what you are referring to. It would also be completely illegal, as the CAN-SPAM Act states it is against the law to intentionally mislead someone with your subject line to induce them to view the message. Let me say this again: IT'S ILLEGAL!

A few other tactics to increase and verify opening rates:

- The aforementioned Yesware research showed that opening rates were highest around 7 AM and 8 PM. While this goes against the old sales rule to contact prospects during business hours, it's possible that prospects are less distracted in the morning, when they browse through their emails after they get up, and at night once the kids are in bed and they settle down on the couch to catch up on emails. You don't even have to stay in the office until 8 PM to send these emails; all email systems these days offer delayed delivery options. (Keep in mind, though, that at both these times, the platform on which your email will be opened is most likely to be a smartphone; see the next section.)

- Use email tracking software like Sidekick or HubSpot to determine if your seed email was opened.
- If you work with senior executives who are well known in the business community or the prospect's category, or might even know prospects personally, don't be shy to ask and get them to send the email for you.

CONVINCE AND CONVERT WITH COMPELLING COPY

Getting prospects to open an email is only the first step in your quest to get them to agree to a face-to-face meeting. Your opening sentence must equally convince, and give them a reason to keep reading. Unfortunately, most of the time it doesn't. In my most recent positions, I have been getting a few dozen emails from potential vendors every week. Most are horrendous and quite frankly an embarrassment to the vendors' companies. It's no surprise, though; writing compelling seed email copy is not easy. And many companies and sales managers don't provide their staff with adequate training for it, if any.

Research has shown consistently in recent years that about four out of five emails are opened on a smartphone and not a desktop/laptop. Take a moment, put the book down, and pick up your smartphone. Open your email in-box and take a look at the last few emails you received from companies, friends, and colleagues. While emails can look different based on the device you are using as well as your personal settings, what you will notice is that you only see the name of the sender, the first few words of the subject line, and the first two lines of the opening sentence. That's it! Even on a laptop, most messages are set up to preview some text, usually one or two lines maximum. You already know an intriguing subject line is important. Start your emails with your strongest line as well.

To write an effective seed email, you need to put yourself into the shoes of prospects and try to relate to their challenges. The last thing they want is another email with a hyperbolic claim about your product or service that is eight paragraphs long. Instead, make your email as short as possible and only as long as necessary. In fact, a great exercise for sales meetings or trainings is to draft your seed email as a text message or tweet. When you first try it, your text likely will be way too long. You would never send a text message like that to someone, right? Reading an email on your smartphone is not that different from reading a text. So keep them short and concise.

One of the best lessons I ever received was to try to write how you speak. That especially applies to writing seed emails. Don't overcomplicate them; make them easy to read. You are not writing a thesis. Prospects are already busy and distracted. Don't create additional work for them by using fancy phrases and complicated sentences.

EFFECTIVE SEED EMAIL FRAMEWORK

Similar to how we provided a framework for a cold call, let's dissect the components of an effective seed email, shown in Figure 9.1.

Let's take a closer look at six of these components.

Greeting

Use only the prospect's first name; this will look professional. No "Dear," "Hi," or "Hello." As with cold calls, "Mr." or "Ms." is overkill and unnecessary.

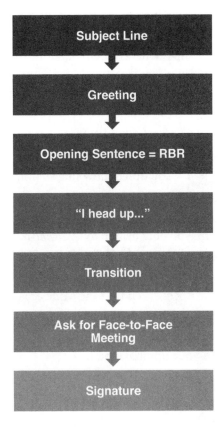

Figure 9.1: Effective Seed Email Framework

Opening Sentence = RBR

We need to come at prospects guns blazing. So don't hold back; start with your RBR. A great RBR is the hook that makes the prospect read on.

I am constantly amazed how weak the openings of many seed emails that I receive are. Here are a few examples for opening lines you should never use:

- *"My name is . . ."* Guess what? Prospects just received an email from you that displayed your name in their in-box. And if they—somehow—missed that part, I am sure your name is

included in your signature at the bottom of the email. Save this
line for your next James Bond impression!

- *"I am with . . ."* Same here. Your email address most likely includes
  the name of the company, as does your signature. Plus, you can
  mention your company in the *"I head up"* part of the email (more
  on this shortly).
- *"Company/Product is the leading/the best/the biggest . . ."* Or some
  other unimportant, navel-gazing crap.
- *"Hope you are well."* You don't know me, so don't pretend as if you
  actually care.
- *"I'm following up on my last email."* In the race for worst seed email
  opening line, maybe only beaten by *"Moving this back to the top of
  your in-box."* All you do is remind prospects that your previous
  email(s) clearly were not compelling enough to elicit a positive
  reaction. No prospect should get the same email twice in one
  Heavy Metal outreach campaign. Come up with something new.
  Use one of the other RBRs you came up with. And certainly don't
  just re-forward your original email.

"I head up . . ."

Just as with a cold call, these three words help to establish authority with
prospects—now that they are at least interested enough to still be reading
the email. Make yourself look like an expert.

Transition

Transitional statement that builds on the RBR and highlights how you are
planning to involve the prospect next; for example:

"I'd love to schedule a video call to help me understand better . . ."
"While I don't know if we are a good fit, why don't we set up . . ."
"From there we can decide if it makes sense to have a deeper conversation."

You are setting up the actual meeting ask.

Ask for the Face-To-Face Meeting

Make it as easy as possible for the prospect to react with a "yes" or "that works." To do that, be very specific with your ask, since—contrary to a cold call—you won't be able to clarify your ask, at least right away. Include the date and time to take the burden about the details off the prospect's shoulders. And definitely specify whether you expect to have a video call or an in-person meeting. If it is the latter, you will need to clarify where: in the prospect's office, your office, or somewhere else.

"Does next Tuesday 4PM at your office work?"

Stay away from inviting prospects you haven't even established a dialogue with to lunch, dinner, or drinks. This was good advice even before COVID-19, and is certainly even more valid now. There will be ample time for that once you have converted the prospect into a client.

Signature

Lead in to your email signature with a line like *"Looking forward to meeting you"* or *"Looking forward to talking with you."* Make sure your email signature is accurate and complete, including first and last name, company name, and your title. Your email signature certainly provides the opportunity to display a tagline or positioning statement, but stay away from company logos or awards. No one cares that you were the number-one salesperson in the Southwest region last year!

Templates Make You More Productive

The benefit of using this seven-step framework is that for several of the components, the actual language won't change that much from prospect to prospect. That's a good thing. There is no need to create every single seed email from scratch. You can find a lot of common ground among your emails, especially within certain categories, that will allow you to create a template prospects will perceive as totally customized when they open the email. Templates boost productivity by making it easy to repurpose some of your previously used wordings. That frees up time you can spend on creating more customized subject lines and opening lines.

One last thing: there is nothing more off-putting than receiving emails full of typos. A seed email also reflects your professionalism. Before you hit the send button, review your email a few more times. Use spell-check or grammarly.com to eliminate spelling or grammar errors. Don't ruin well-thought-out sentences with sloppy typos.

CASE STUDY: SEED EMAIL TO REBECCA GYMS

For the seed email to Rebecca Gyms CMO Tracy Ranner, you decide to use the Insight RBR you developed earlier. Here is the email broken down into its seven components, following our framework:

Step 1—Subject Line:
1.1m NYC women don't go to gyms

Step 2—Greeting:
Tracy,

Step 3—Opening Sentence:

Sixty-seven percent of New York women between the ages of 25 and 49 don't belong to a gym. That's a pool of 1.1m potential members for Rebecca Gyms.

Step 4:
I head up the Health and Fitness vertical at NYC Media in New York.

Step 5—Transition:

We have tons of detailed market segmentation data like this, which will prove helpful for your launch here. Why don't we schedule some time for you and I to go over and learn more about your upcoming New York plans. From there we can decide if it makes sense to have a deeper conversation.

Step 6—Ask for Meeting:
Does next Monday at 2 PM EST work for a video call?

Step 7—Signature:
Please let me know. Looking forward to speaking with you.

The entire seed email would look like this:

Subject: 1.1m NYC women don't go to gyms

Tracy,

Sixty-seven percent of New York women between the ages of 25 and 49 don't belong to a gym. That's a pool of 1.1m potential members for Rebecca Gyms.

I head up the Health and Fitness vertical at NYC Media in New York. We have tons of detailed market segmentation data like this, which will prove helpful for your launch here. Why don't we schedule some time for you and I to go over and learn more about your upcoming New York plans. From there we can decide if it makes sense to have a deeper conversation.

Does next Monday 2 PM EST work for a video call?

Please let me know. Looking forward to speaking with you.

Dave Gahan
Account Executive
NYC Media

Using the Introduction RBR—our LA acquaintance—the seed email could look like this:

Subject: Rob Meyers said we should talk

Tracy,

Rob Meyers at RMS Agency suggested we should connect on Rebecca Gyms' planned New York expansion. The two of us worked together on several successful marketing projects in the Northeast.

I head up the Health and Fitness vertical at NYC Media in New York. Why don't we set up some time for you and me to connect to learn more about your upcoming plans here. I can share some case studies of comparable launch campaigns we have worked on, and from there we can decide if it makes sense to have a deeper conversation.

Does next Monday early afternoon work for a video call? Maybe 2 PM EST?

Please let me know. Looking forward to speaking with you.

Using the In-Segment Success Story RBR, an effective seed email would be:

Subject: Lessons learned from Y7 Studio NYC launch

Tracy,

We recently helped Y7 Studio launch ten new locations here in New York. And as a result, they surpassed their membership goals by 43 percent.

I head up the Health and Fitness vertical at NYC Media and wanted to share with you what exactly worked for them and show you some potential learnings for your upcoming launch in New York. While I can't be certain at this point if we are a good fit for Rebecca Gyms, why don't we schedule a video call to help me learn more about your plans and challenges. From there we can decide if it makes sense to have a deeper conversation.

Does next Monday early afternoon work for you? Maybe 2 PM?

Please let me know. Looking forward to speaking with you.

A seed email using the Idea RBR could look like this:

Subject: Rebecca Gyms launches fitness movement

Tracy,

Imagine if we created a movement of New York women who hold each other accountable to work out on a regular basis. A movement that is led by our female radio personalities and bloggers.

I head up the Health and Fitness vertical at NYC Media and wanted to schedule a video call to share a few more details on this idea. Would also love to hear more about your plans for your upcoming launch in New York. From there we can decide if it makes sense to have a deeper conversation.

Does next Monday at 2 PM EST work for a video call?

Please let me know. Looking forward to speaking next week.

10

PERFECTING LINKEDIN MESSAGES

eed emails and LinkedIn messages are closely related. For example, a good Relevant Business Reason is as important in a LinkedIn message as it is in a seed email. LinkedIn messages also need to start strong and have a specific call to action, all things we covered in the previous chapter on seed emails.

However, you need to be aware of some differences. For example, LinkedIn messages need to be even shorter than seed emails. At the time of writing, you are only allowed three hundred characters when reaching out with a customized message to connect with a prospect, only 86 of which can initially be seen by prospects, who have to actively click on "see more" to view your entire message. This customized message to connect should be a short version of your RBR.

Getting connected with your prospect on LinkedIn means you now have permission to follow up with sales and marketing messages. As a next step, you send a follow-up message to ask them for a face-to-face meeting. Again, your message has to be very concise. When sending messages to prospects with whom you are already connected, the recipient's cursor in the browser version of LinkedIn will often automatically jump to the bottom of the received message—to the reply field—which can cut off the top of your message if it is too long, forcing prospects to manually scroll up to see the beginning. Since you can't bank on them actually doing that, try to keep your message to eight lines or less.

PROFILE PICTURE AND HEADLINE

Consider treating your LinkedIn messages like short text messages and use abbreviations, numbers, and symbols to keep them short. The good news is that you don't need to include a signature at the bottom of your message like you would when sending emails. The prospect will see your profile picture, name, and LinkedIn headline when your message comes through. If you needed an additional reason to make sure these items look professional, this is it.

I am constantly stunned by the type of pictures some salespeople use on LinkedIn: some showing them doing shots with the company mascot, others posing in shorts on the beach. Use whatever you want on Facebook and other social sites, but your LinkedIn profile picture needs to be as professional looking as possible. If you currently don't show a profile picture, upload one. Prospects want to see a picture of you.

Choose your LinkedIn headline strategically. It should include your job title and the name of your company. If you decide to add some type of positioning statement, my choice would be to make it more about yourself than your employer. Too many salespeople think this is a great place to brag that their company is the biggest, best, or boldest. It is not. Prospects will have the same negative reaction they have when you use "salesy" language in seed emails.

TAKING ADVANTAGE OF INMAIL MESSAGES

You have more space to write when using InMail messages in LinkedIn, but these require you to have one of LinkedIn's premium subscriptions. InMail messages should follow the structure of seed emails described in the previous chapter. They even allow you to include subject lines, which the other LinkedIn messages mentioned do not. And InMail messages also pop up in your prospect's email in-box, which is a huge advantage.

NOT EVERYBODY IS ON LINKEDIN EVERY DAY

You also have to be aware that every time you send a LinkedIn message, you are piling onto the last message you sent. That's something you have to take into account when you send follow-up messages. What if your prospect hasn't even seen the first message you sent yet? With LinkedIn, response times can be slower than with regular seed emails. While it certainly has become a widely used tool, LinkedIn's heaviest users are salespeople, recruiters, and job seekers. Don't expect decision makers to spend time on the platform every day. As a result, it could be days, sometimes weeks, until you hear back. That is another reason to spread out messages more than with emails. The last thing you want is for your prospects to check their LinkedIn messages only to find three of yours on top of each other.

Nevertheless, LinkedIn messages can help you bypass the gatekeeper to C-suite executives (assistants, secretaries, etc.), who often have access to the decision maker's company email in-box to weed out solicitations, but not to their LinkedIn accounts.

CASE STUDY:
LINKEDIN MESSAGE TO REBECCA GYMS' CHIEF MARKETING OFFICER

You want to connect with CMO Tracy Ranner on LinkedIn and send her an invitation, including a customized note.

Tracy, we recently helped Y7 Studio launch 10 new locations in NYC. They surpassed their membership goals by 43 percent. I would love to share our strategy & get to know more about Rebecca Gyms. Looking forward to connecting!

Once Tracy accepts your invitation, you follow up with a short message to ask for the meeting:

Tracy, thank you for connecting. I see that Rebecca Gyms will be expanding to New York—would love to dive into this further. Does next Monday at 2 PM EST work for a video call?

11

OTHER WAYS TO GET IN THE DOOR

Reaching out by phone, email, and LinkedIn are not the only ways for salespeople to set up face-to-face meetings with new business prospects.

SUCCEEDING WITH SOCIAL SELLING

Many, many books and articles have been written on "social selling," a vague term that, for our purposes, we'll define as "using social media platforms to generate sales." While we can't cover all the details in this book, it makes sense to review the tactics that sales champions have adopted in the social media space over the last few years.

The term "social selling" itself is certainly misleading. From a B2B sales perspective, reaching out to a prospect actively on LinkedIn, either through an InMail message or simply by first connecting and then reaching out with a follow-up message, does fall into the "sales" bucket. We covered this tactic in the previous chapter. However, most other activities—like posting articles or sharing research studies—are much closer to marketing than sales. You're marketing your company, and, even more so, yourself. There's nothing wrong with that, of course. A company's effective sales marketing strategy can make life much easier for its sales force. Prospects become more familiar with the company's brand and its offerings, and its salespeople don't need to start from scratch when speaking with prospects by explaining what the company does and stands for.

Social media and especially a platform like LinkedIn can absolutely help you become a more effective seller. In fact, failure to engage in social selling will put you at a massive disadvantage to others that do. LinkedIn is especially effective in deepening relationships with existing clients, since you can see all of their connections and use them to improve your depth of contact, including potential influencers you have not met. Similarly, posting an article of value will make an impression with your client and potentially benefit you.

Social Selling Alone Is Not Enough

The issues begin when salespeople—especially younger ones, who grew up on social media and are certainly much more knowledgeable and experienced in it than someone closer to my own age—think that social selling is *all* they have to do to get in the door with prospects. It almost sounds too good to be true, right? Instead of being rejected over the phone, instead of being rained on while doing in-person walk-ins, instead of waiting for your voicemail to be returned—all you need to do is create a brand for yourself in the social space. And once your name has become familiar with decision makers, you simply wait for them to reach out to you and ask you for a meeting or, even better, a proposal.

Unfortunately, it doesn't work like that. Sorry. Social selling is not the panacea many will try to make you believe it is. I have yet to meet the salesperson who was able to consistently generate enough leads to make budget without any type of other outreach method. Look at it as just one more weapon in your outreach arsenal, not the only one.

Limit Your Social Selling Time

Personal branding in sales is not a new concept. Almost twenty years ago, when selling radio in New York, I had my own personal website: radio advertising.fm. It included facts about radio advertising, tips for effective ad copy, success stories, and even a weekly newsletter for prospects and clients. It certainly made me stand out in the marketplace, since no other radio seller in the market had anything like it. It impressed new prospects and helped me create additional touchpoints with existing clients. It also gave me a lot of self-confidence. There were many positives, but I eventually gave up curating it; maintaining the site and keeping the content consistently fresh simply took too much time.

That's one of the biggest issues with social selling: doing it effectively takes a lot of time. That time could have been used for proactive selling, like cold calling or meeting prospects.

Don't get me wrong. I like social. I am seeing success with it. So are many salespeople I know. But my advice to newer salespeople is to be disciplined about it and limit your "personal branding" time on LinkedIn to one hour per week max. Ideally, that hour is not a prime selling hour. Post, share, connect as much as you want during these sixty minutes, but once the hour is over, move on to a more productive activity.

LinkedIn is the most widely used social media platform for social selling. We already covered how to successfully use LinkedIn messages as a weapon in your sales arsenal. The following are some additional best practices on how to take advantage of LinkedIn to generate new business:

Proactively Increase Referrals and Introductions

Nothing works better than referrals and introductions. In chapter seven we covered the importance of checking mutual LinkedIn connections to determine who could potentially make an introduction for you, or at least give you more information about a prospect. I am mentioning this here again because it is so important. While checking for mutuals is not a new strategy, LinkedIn has made it easier than ever.

Personal Branding: Content Creation, Curation, and Distribution

This is the portion of social selling that can easily take over your workday, and that's why it's important to set a time limit.

Posting content on LinkedIn is a great way to stay in front of your customers and prospects. Determine your best strategy to stay consistently visible without spending hours and hours on creating content from scratch. Find the right mix between sharing information that you think may be relevant and educational for your connections and publishing your own articles, presentations, or studies. Sharing positive news about you and your company is absolutely allowed—but occasionally. Salespeople who only post self-promotional material get ignored very quickly.

Personal branding and content creation or curation are especially important for salespeople who work for less-well-known companies, including start-ups and smaller firms that cannot rely on a big corporate marketing machine to generate buzz. LinkedIn is an effective tool to increase familiarity with your company: the more you can help do so, the easier it will be to get new prospects to meet with you.

Inbound Lead Generation

Sharing relevant news and posting educational content can entice prospects to proactively contact you. Obviously, that is the best-case scenario in a new business development role, since it is much easier to set up a meeting with an inbound lead than by making an outbound cold call. Make sure you research the person and company that reached out to determine if it is a qualified lead worth your time.

A more active way to generate inbound leads is to host webinars and post white papers and e-books that require prospects to enter their contact information to access the content. Most of the time, though, this will be part of a more coordinated effort by your company or sales team, since efforts like this can become very time consuming on the front and back ends.

THE LOST ART OF IN-PERSON WALK-INS

There was a time when dropping in to businesses and offices unannounced was the method of outreach salespeople spent the most time on. Sales teams across the world were told to "not be seen in the office between 9 AM and 4 PM." That, of course, suited many salespeople perfectly well. After all, out in the field, on your own, you are less accountable than when cold-calling in the office.

Of all the possible outreach channels, walk-ins are by far the most inefficient. You can cold-call or email twenty prospects in the time you'd spend driving to a business miles away, in the hope you might find the prospect there in person. Up until a few years ago I thought salespeople spent too much time on this in-person prospecting method. More recently, however, I have noticed that salespeople are not doing enough of it. Done effectively, walk-ins complement other outreach methods perfectly. They are another weapon in your Heavy Metal outreach arsenal.

Walk-Ins Take Preparation

To make walk-ins successful, it's essential to prepare yourself. It's pointless to drive around aimlessly for an entire day and not get anything done. Instead, you need to plan your day and determine who you will see.

Plot out the prospects you are planning to see, determine the quickest route to get there, and make their locations the "anchors" of your selling day. They have priority. After all, these prospects wouldn't be on your lead list if you didn't at least suspect they were good leads; you simply have not been successful in setting up meetings with them over the phone or by email.

Once you reach the client's office, don't stop there. Look around. Is there another business in the area that looks intriguing? If there is, stop in, gather intelligence, and determine if you should invest further time in this company. This activity is more prospecting work than connecting work.

Combining existing prospects that serve as anchors with potential new prospects you find along the way is the only efficient way to approach in-person walk-ins. It works, and you should make use of it. Some prospects simply cannot be reached by phone or email. You will be surprised how many doors in-person walk-ins will literally open for you.

Most businesses won't have the red carpet rolled out for you. In fact, quite the opposite. You might even see a "no soliciting" sign on the door. But don't let that deter you. Approach with a confident smile, introduce yourself, and ask for the decision maker. It's not much different from a cold call except that you are doing it in person. Because of that, since most people will be a little more helpful than they are over the phone, your conversion rate will be higher.

Relevant Business Reasons Don't Change with Walk-Ins

The goal of a walk-in is the same as the goal of a cold call or seed email: to set up a face-to-face meeting with the decision maker. Most of the time, that meeting will be scheduled for a future date. Once in a while—especially when you work in an industry like pharma or automotive—the meeting will take place right then and there.

The RBRs you developed as part of your Heavy Metal outreach strategy—an idea, an In-Segment Success Story, an insight, or an introduction—don't change when you are physically in front of prospects. The only difference is that they are now delivered in person. Of course, the message will sound a little different than it does over the phone, but the core reasons you are giving prospects for meeting with you stay the same.

Reviewing your CRM and your research notes the day before, or in the morning before you head out, is essential so you can remember RBRs and facts about prospects. You would be surprised how often I have witnessed salespeople, who I knew had come up with several good RBRs in preparation for a cold-call session, suddenly revert to the dreaded "I want to talk to you about your advertising" during walk-ins. If you deliver your RBRs well, you will even find that objections will be easier to handle in person.

If the buyer wants to meet with you on the spot, go for it. Just make sure you are prepared and have some relevant case studies or insights ready. Then proceed with a needs analysis. Ask questions about the buyer's challenges and plans, and keep qualifying. This is good news; just don't act overtly surprised it is happening. Make it look as if you expected it and determine whether your company and the prospect are a good fit to start a deeper conversation.

If the decision maker is not available, you definitely want to have some leave-behind material with you. What I have found effective is a one-page showcasing companies in the area or category in which you're working (*"A Snapshot of Our Partners in the Bronx"*), combined with a handwritten message and your business card. Leave it with the receptionist, secretary, or assistant, but only after you asked to find out who else they'd suggest you should meet. This is a great way to uncover the names of other influencers and even decision makers. And, of course, it's a great opportunity to make friends with gatekeepers. Make sure to capture everyone's name, including all gatekeepers', in your CRM when you are back at the office.

SETTING UP MEETINGS BY THINKING OUT OF THE BOX

One of my favorite exercises with sales teams is to write down *"cold call," "seed email," "LinkedIn,"* and *"in-person"* on a whiteboard and then ask people to just call out additional ways for them to set up meetings with new business prospects. For about thirty seconds, it's usually quiet. Then one salesperson will come up with an out-of-the-box idea, and five minutes later the whiteboard is full, with at least a dozen additional get-in-the-door tactics.

I once worked with a very talented salesperson who thought she had tried everything humanly possible to set up a meeting with the regional marketing director of a global bank. For months she got no response, despite many, many attempts. Then she somehow found out that this prospect was an avid rock climber. This creative seller then invested fifteen dollars in a rock-climbing rope and sent it to the prospect by mail, with a handwritten note that said *"Erica, would love to 'hook' up and talk about how we can take (name of bank) to new heights."* She got a call back two days later, with a compliment on her creativity, and a high-six-figure deal not long after.

DON'T ABANDON GOOD LEADS TOO QUICKLY

But what if none of your outreach efforts trigger any response from the prospect over these two weeks of Heavy Metal outreach? Do you discard the lead and move on?

You don't move on after just a single two-week get-in-the-door campaign, especially if you feel strongly about the quality of the lead. While each situation is unique, you have several different options:

- Try to find a different way into the company by reaching out to another (or several other) person at the company.
- Hit the pause button for thirty to sixty days, after which you actively start reaching out again, with a second Heavy Metal outreach campaign. In the interim, make sure these prospects are included in your or your company's email distribution list, so they at least receive some information from you.
- Continue right away with another Heavy Metal outreach campaign to the same person. Reasons might include an important deadline coming up on the prospect's side, such as a hard date for a prospect's annual marketing plan, or maybe because you sense the prospect might have missed your earlier messages. You don't want to rely on your original RBRs for the new campaign, though. Come up with a couple of new ones. Maybe the prospect just didn't find your old RBRs compelling enough to engage with you.

If the lack of response continues over several months, you need to evaluate whether the lead should remain on your active lead list. I know how hard it is to walk away from what you think is a monster lead—and usually I am actually more concerned that salespeople abandon a good lead too quickly—but part of smart salesmanship is also to let go when it's time. If a prospect totally ignores you, despite your best outreach efforts over several months, walk away. The only thing you are doing is wasting time that you could spend more productively with other leads.

12

NAVIGATING FOUR POSSIBLE CALL OUTCOMES

S taying with our tennis analogy from earlier in the section, the serving players in tennis face several possible scenarios. They might win the point outright, by hitting an ace or by their opponent missing the return. Or they might get an easy second shot they can convert into a winner, either at the net or by hitting a groundstroke. Their opponents could also hit very strong returns that put the server on the defensive, making it harder to recover from and get back into a rally. And doubles players will have to factor in their second opponents at the net, by either hitting around the net players or engaging them head-on. Sound familiar?

When cold-calling a new business prospect, you also need to navigate several different possible situations that can broadly be categorized into four outcomes, summarized in Figure 12.1:

1. Your prospect agrees to the face-to-face meeting right away
2. Your prospect doesn't pick up the phone
3. You are routed to a gatekeeper
4. Your prospect voices one—or several—objections

The fact that you are interrupting someone's busy schedule with a phone call he or she was not expecting—and in that second most likely didn't want to receive—means that the cards are not stacked in your favor. Of the four possible outcomes, the one where you walk prospects through your Relevant Business Reason, and they are so immediately impressed by it that they suggest scheduling a meeting, is in the clear minority. If that wasn't the case, cold-calling reluctance would probably not exist.

Figure 12.1: Four Possible Scenarios of a Cold Call

YOUR PROSPECT SAYS YES

The buyer picked up the phone, and you had chosen the right RBR that interested the prospect enough to agree to meet with you face to face, either on a video call or in person. You would think it's easy from here, and it should be. However, I have observed too many salespeople talk themselves out of a meeting the prospect had already agreed to. That's why I must caution you unequivocally:

GET . . . OFF . . . THE . . . PHONE!

Right after your qualified prospect agreed to meet with you is *not* the right time to start asking questions. There is no need to start a mini

discovery meeting over the phone. You will be able to do that more effectively in person, in what will be a much more relaxed atmosphere. Remember, you just interrupted the prospect only a couple of minutes earlier. It's
also not the right time to start talking about how great your company,
product, or service is or to go into details about how the idea you just presented as part of your RBR will work. Clearly, you already intrigued the
person on the other line enough to score the meeting. Hold these details
until your face-to-face meeting.

Coordinate the Meeting

All you have to do after the prospect's *yes* is to agree to the exact date,
time, and place of the meeting. If the meeting is with a prospect who is
not located in your time zone, make sure to confirm the time. You should
also always clarify whether you are meeting in person or on a video or
conference call.

If your company has an office built to impress, potentially even cen-
trally located and easy for your prospect to reach, and you can convince
them to meet you there, you will have an advantage. An office tour, including an introduction to senior executives or—if you work in media—even
well-known on-air personalities, can be a great icebreaker with someone
you are meeting for the first time and will go a long way toward establishing rapport with the prospect.

Regardless of how you will meet, after you verify the prospect's contact information, including email address and direct office line, make sure
to ask, *"Is there anyone else on your end who should be in the meeting?"* Then get
those people's email addresses as well.

Send a Meeting Invitation

Once you get off the phone, send a meeting invitation to all attendees,
including the location of the meeting or video call details. I use the subject
line *"Name of prospect* and *Name of your company* Partnership Meeting (or

Video Call)." In our case study of Rebecca Gyms, the subject line on the Outlook invitation would say *"Rebecca Gyms and NYC Media Partnership Video Call."*

The length of the meeting in the invitation will vary by industry. As mentioned, I personally prefer forty-five minutes. I also try to schedule more face-to-face meetings on Tuesdays, Wednesdays, and Thursdays and fewer on Mondays and Fridays. Why? Because at this point in the sales process, when you have no personal relationship with the prospect, new business meetings are usually the first to get canceled or rescheduled, and the risk of this happening on a day right before or after the weekend is higher in my experience.

Send Confirmation Email

Some salespeople are hesitant to confirm new business meetings with prospects a day in advance, thinking that reminding them of the meeting might actually result in the opposite: a request to reschedule, or—even worse—a cancellation. I never bought into this theory. If you want to come across as a professional businessperson, confirming your meeting a day in advance will show prospects that you consider your own time at least as precious as theirs.

If your meeting will be conducted via video call, remind the prospect of that. The last thing you want is your meeting to turn into a basic conference call, making it harder for you to build a relationship and impossible to share information on a screen.

Consider giving the prospect a pre-meeting assignment. Nothing major, of course, but you could assign something that is just enough to get the person involved in the process even before you meet face to face. You might ask the prospect to read a relevant article. Or you could mention certain things in your meeting confirmation email you are planning to cover during the meeting, with the expectation that the prospect give them some thought before the meeting. A prepared prospect is a better prospect. But you need to *ask* the person to prepare. Odds are they won't do it on their own.

CASE STUDY:
CONFIRMATION EMAIL TO REBECCA GYMS

Here is how a confirmation email to Tracy Ranner, chief marketing officer of Rebecca Gyms, might look:

Hi, Tracy,

I am looking forward to our video call tomorrow at 2 PM. I have done as much research as I could on Rebecca Gyms in preparation for our meeting, but do have a few more questions about your marketing strategy and plans that I wanted to go over on the call. I want to make sure I 100 percent understand what your needs, challenges, and KPIs are. I am also planning to share some relevant case studies and category insights as well as NYC Media's analytics tools.

I added a Microsoft Teams link to the invite for you to easily access the video call (no need to install anything, though; all you need to do is click the link). Please feel free to invite anyone else on your team who you think should be part of our call.

Talk to (and see) you tomorrow.

VOICEMAILS ARE PART OF YOUR SALES CAMPAIGN

We have all been there before. We have all questioned if leaving voicemails is really worth it:

"It's just a waste of time."

"Nobody ever calls me back."

"I don't think people are even listening to voicemail."

"The more voicemails I leave with the same prospect, the more of a pest I become."

For years I struggled over whether to leave voice messages. There certainly was a time in my sales career when I decided against them. My main argument was that I didn't want to block myself from cold-calling a prospect again during my next cold-call session (either the same or the next day). I felt that leaving a voicemail in the morning and following up with another call in the afternoon would be interpreted as overly aggressive if the prospect picked up the second call. Then it occurred to me one day that no prospect actually ever complained about it. Way more often, they apologized for not getting back to me.

Voicemails as Short Radio Commercials

What really changed my mind over time was when I started to think about voicemails less as a vehicle to get people to call me back, and more as a tool to deliver one additional sales and marketing impression to a prospect. Working in the radio industry, I started to look at voicemail messages as fifteen- to twenty-second-long radio commercials. And, much as I might achieve with a radio commercial, I figured the awareness and familiarity of me and the company I was representing would increase with every additional voicemail impression.

I also stopped looking at not receiving a call back as a failure or setback. I expected it. It didn't bother me, because my overall goal—to set up a face-to-face meeting with the prospect—remained the same. Whether I achieved it because prospects ended up responding to a seed email I sent after hearing my voicemail didn't matter to me. I looked at it as one comprehensive Heavy Metal outreach campaign, two weeks long, with different tactics that complemented each other. We all know that it takes a number of touches to break through. Voicemails are just one more of them.

This doesn't mean you should leave a voicemail every time you are calling a prospect. As you have already seen, a two-week outreach campaign includes three to four voicemails. This number is only reasonable if you switch up your voicemail message accordingly, using different RBRs, to stay engaging. Otherwise you will very quickly become a pest.

That said, there is no doubt that leaving voicemails or—more accurately—waiting for call backs can be frustrating. So is the fact that many decision makers rarely pick up the phone in the first place, sending the majority of cold calls to voicemail. But is voicemail less effective now than a decade ago? I don't believe so. The fact that these days, audio files of your voicemails are being forwarded to a buyer's email in-box, actually helps you, because prospects will receive voicemails faster, and your chances of them actually listening to your message are higher.

In certain industries (e.g., technology) and at start-ups with many younger buyers, you might find it a bit harder to get a call returned. You will encounter voice messages like *"I am not listening to voicemail"* more often, or situations when you literally can't leave a voicemail because the buyer's in-box is full. Some buyers will just think that if a salesperson has a really important reason to call, they will try again soon—and as a result, the buyers won't call back themselves.

Having the Right Voicemail Mindset

For voicemail, as with any outreach method, perseverance will make the difference and maximize your chances of getting a call back. Shift your mindset to *"Voicemail is a real weapon for me."* Embrace it, be positive about it. Make sure your energy level is high and don't come across like someone who is just doing a job. Never get angry and show frustration. It will never help you.

The only time I would recommend easing up on voicemail is when prospects change their voicemail to an out-of-office or vacation message. You don't want them to come back to work checking tons of voicemail messages from different vendors, with your voicemail stuck somewhere between the sixteenth and the nineteenth messages, never to be fully heard.

It is totally fine to include some humor, especially after several outreach attempts haven't resulted in a call back. I once met a salesperson who, after a few weeks of leaving voicemails with the same prospect, would leave one that mentioned something like *"Every time before I go to bed I talk to God, why can't I talk to you?"* Will this work for every sales style? Of course not. But figure out what type of humor could work for you, and use it in the right situation. It's much better than sounding too polished or like a telemarketing robot.

Lastly, make sure your phone connection is up to standard and that your message will come across clearly. It is mind-boggling how often I receive voicemails that I want to understand but simply can't, because they were left from someone's cell phone while the caller was walking in windy weather outside or was calling from a car. Leave your outreach voicemails from your office phone.

Voicemails Must Be Short

So what should an effective voicemail include? Essentially, what you would say if you had the prospect on the phone live, just shorter. Plus, make it as easy as possible for the prospect to call you back.

Your message needs to stand out. Stick to one of the RBRs you came up with during your prep work, and focus on the most relevant part of it. Think of how you tease an email with a concise and effective subject line, or how you shorten your RBR for a LinkedIn message. Some salespeople go on and on for over a minute, which is bad salesmanship in general, but even worse when the buyer gets the voicemail forwarded to their email, where the length of the audio file is visible. Anything longer than thirty seconds screams "DELETE!" before they even start listening. And, worse than deleting it, the buyer will remember it was you who left that lengthy message.

Your voicemail should under no circumstances be longer than twenty seconds. Sometimes salespeople say that's just not possible. My answer: the Pledge of Allegiance is shorter than that. Are you saying your message is more important than the Pledge of Allegiance? Brevity with voicemail is key. There should be no wasted words, no long transitioning to what you want to accomplish, no job titles. Like Mark

Hunter writes in *High-Profit Prospecting*, "Do you think the other person cares you're a 'Vice-President of the North-South District in the Western Region?'" Well said.

Include Your Call-Back Number Three Times

Include your call-back number once at the beginning of the voicemail, so prospects don't have to play back the entire message once they decide to

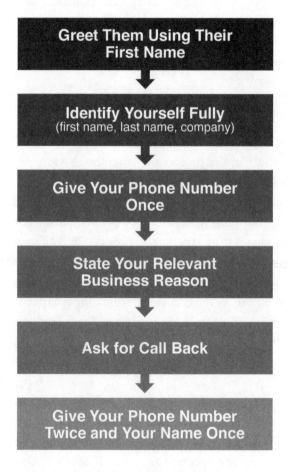

Figure 12.2: Effective Voicemail Framework

call you back. Then include it twice more at the end of your message. You will need to decide if it makes more sense to give your office number or cell phone number; what's better for you depends on your particular setup. I leave my cell phone number simply because I am on the road a lot and want to maximize my chances to be able to pick up a return call.

Effective Voicemail Framework

Similar to how we broke down cold calls and seed emails into their components, Figure 12.2 shows the framework of an effective voicemail message.

As with cold calls, it's perfectly acceptable to write a precise voicemail script in preparation. If you're not comfortable working with scripts, you should at least write down quick talking points. Then practice, practice, practice! With voicemails, that's actually very easy to do. Leave yourself a voicemail and listen to it. Chances are you'll hear something that you can improve on. Have a coworker listen to it. Time it. You will be surprised how long messages actually are, even if you told yourself to be concise several times before you picked up the phone.

One last lesson on voicemails: always enter the RBR you used into your CRM, and be prepared when your prospect calls back. That's often easier said than done, since you probably have left several voicemails with different companies using various RBRs over a short time. It can get confusing. You have to be able to think quickly on your feet, especially if you get the call back on your cell phone and are not at your desk.

CASE STUDY:
VOICEMAIL SCRIPT FOR REBECCA GYMS

Here is a potential voicemail message to Rebecca Gyms CMO Tracy Ranner, broken down into its components.

Step 1—Greeting:
"Tracy,"

Step 2—Identification:
"this is Dave Gahan with NYC Media,"

Step 3—Phone Number:
"at 646-765-XXXX."

Step 4—RBR:
"We recently helped Y7 Studio launch their ten new locations here in New York. And as a result, they surpassed their membership goals by 43 percent."

Step 5—Ask for Call Back:
"I'd love to share some potential learnings for your upcoming New York launch."

Step 6—Name and Phone Number:
"Tracy, please give me a call at 646-765-XXXX. Again, this is Dave Gahan, NYC Media, 646-765-XXXX."

The entire voicemail script would therefore look like this:

"Tracy, this is Dave Gahan with NYC Media, at 646-765-XXXX. We recently helped Y7 Studio launch their ten new locations here in New York. And as a result, they surpassed their membership goals by 43 percent. I'd love to share some potential learnings for your upcoming New York launch. Tracy, please give me a call at 646-765-XXXX. Again, this is Dave Gahan, NYC Media, 646-765-XXXX."

BEFRIENDING GATEKEEPERS

Most salespeople have a negative reaction when they hear the word "gatekeeper." Who can blame them? It's not like gatekeepers have endeared themselves to the sales profession over the last few decades. They certainly can become obstacles, standing in the way of a meeting with a buyer.

"If it weren't for the gatekeeper blocking me, I would have already made the sale" is something we've probably all told ourselves at one time. However, sales champions consistently find a way to engage gatekeepers in the sales process, potentially even turning them into allies and internal coaches along the way.

How are they doing it? They are ultimately just following advice they first received when they were about six years old, and their mothers told them to treat every human being with the utmost respect. Yes, gatekeepers are people like you and me, with real lives, emotions, and problems of their own. They are just trying to get their jobs done, like you. They can have a variety of roles, from the executive assistant who knows the company's strategy and secrets better than anyone else, to the receptionist who was told not to let any salespeople walk by the reception desk. All of them have one thing in common: they want to protect their bosses, or, more specifically, their bosses' time.

Be Open and Transparent with Gatekeepers

The best way to engage gatekeepers is to be friendly and start a conversation with them. You want to establish a dialogue that—in a best-case scenario—eventually turns them into your friend and helper. For this relationship to get off to a good start, you have to be as transparent about your intentions as possible from the beginning. Be up front about who you are and where you are calling from. I have met many salespeople over the years who were proud of their long list of tricks to *get past the gatekeeper.* In the end, these just made them look like, well, salespeople. Not to mention that the vast majority of times these tricks backfired on them and did nothing else but hurt their credibility.

If you are not transparent off the bat, the gatekeeper will absolutely ask you the dreaded question, *"What's this in regard to?"* Instead of getting defensive and potentially even trying to intimidate and almost "demand" the meeting, you shouldn't be in this position in the first place. Treat gatekeepers as if they are the decision makers, using the cold-call script with the RBRs you had prepared in advance.

Two things will happen:

1. The gatekeeper will feel honored or at least thankful for being treated with respect.
2. If your RBR was strong enough, the gatekeeper will be hesitant to turn down what could be a great opportunity for the manager and the company, and will try to minimize her personal risk by actually putting you through.

Turning Gatekeepers into Allies

If the buyer is not available, use the conversation you started with the gatekeeper to your advantage. You can gain many insights by simply asking for help and guidance.

"When is the best time to reach her?"

"What would you suggest is the best way to earn forty-five minutes on his schedule?"

"Who else within the company should I be speaking to about this?"

"Do you ever need tickets to a Yankees game?"

I am adding the last question partly in jest, but don't forget gatekeepers are people who have needs. If you have access to tickets to events, concerts, or theme parks, as many salespeople do, why wouldn't you want to offer them? I have had gatekeepers call my cell phone to let me know the buyer was now back in the office and had no meetings scheduled for the next couple of hours. Of course I jumped in the car and made my way there immediately, dropping off a pair of Mets tickets with the gatekeeper along the way.

You can absolutely develop real and positive relationships with gatekeepers before meeting the decision maker. If you did a good job with it, you will have gained a lot of information that will make your first meeting with the buyer so much more productive. Just don't forget about the gatekeeper once you start working directly with the buyer. Nurture this relationship as much as the one with the client. Many salespeople write handwritten thank-you notes to their clients. Try the same with gatekeepers and see what it will do for you.

How to Work Around Them

If you come across gatekeepers who—despite all your efforts and best intentions—simply do not want to connect you or help you in any way, try to work around them:

- Most gatekeepers work traditional hours, so calling between 7 AM and 8 AM, during the lunch hour, or between 6 PM and 7 PM might get you directly to the buyer, or at least to a different person who might be more accommodating.
- Try calling the sales department or the accounts receivable department, a tactic we already introduced when we were trying to determine the right phone number to call during the prospecting phase. Salespeople love to talk; they might even identify with your struggles to set up a meeting and help you out of courtesy. The accounts receivable department is eager to collect money and someone is usually picking up the phone. Ask to be connected, and there is a good chance the person on the other line will pick up.
- As mentioned, gatekeepers usually don't have access to their managers' LinkedIn accounts. This outreach tactic can be especially useful in situations where the decision maker is fully walled off from calls or in-person walk-ins.

DISMISSALS, OBJECTIONS, AND WHAT TO DO ABOUT THEM

In chapter one we covered how sales champions deal with rejection. While rejection can happen at any time in the sales process, there are two steps along the way when it happens the most. One is toward the end, when you are trying to finalize a deal and your prospect rejects your proposal. The other time is when you actually get buyers on the phone during a cold call and they reject your request to meet face to face.

The feeling of rejection happens the moment you get a dismissal or objection (we will get to the difference between these two shortly). And yes, it sucks! Whether you are a sales veteran with thirty years' experience or a twenty-two-year-old in your first sales role, it will throw you a little off your sales game. The key, though, is what you do next. Do you back down immediately and agree to *"call back in six months"*? Do you ask if *"it's okay to check back in a few weeks"*? Or do you stand your ground and—in a calm and professional manner—insist on the meeting, maybe even push back a little? Sales champions do the latter. If there is a time in the entire sales process when it is okay to be a little pushy, this is it. That's why we labeled the Connect phase "Heavy Metal Sales." If you want to think Metallica, now is the time.

But who can blame prospects for rejecting us? For years they have been getting tortured by salespeople who don't provide any value and are only talking about how great they and their companies are. No wonder people are programmed to put us off and reject us. It's almost a reflex. Just think about your own reaction when you get a cold call from someone you don't know. You are being interrupted and all you want to do is get back to whatever you were doing.

Be Ready for Resistance

There are several strategies and tactics you can adopt to improve your odds of successfully getting past a dismissal or an objection. Above all, you need to be prepared. That should be a no-brainer, but based on how I hear salespeople responding every day to objections or dismissals on the phone, it clearly is not.

There are fewer than a dozen ways for a prospect to tell you *no* on a cold call. You would think that you can learn a dozen different responses by heart, wouldn't you? You can and you should, but maybe one out of ten salespeople actually do. We will cover script suggestions later in the chapter to do exactly that. Learn them by heart or come up with your own responses and learn them. The point is, you need to be prepared to respond to an objection or dismissal almost automatically, without awkward pauses or trying to search for the right words.

If you know in advance that you will run into resistance—and you do—there is no reason not to be ready for it. Be ready to push past it with rehearsed scripts, and keep your eye on the goal: getting the face-to-face meeting. If you don't get the meeting, your cold call was not successful. It's as simple as that. Be brutally honest with yourself.

Only that mindset, combined with the willingness to be persistent and to ask for the meeting several times on the same call if necessary, will bring you success. At that moment you will need to have not just one, but several RBRs at your fingertips.

What you are selling at this moment is the meeting. You need to make clear that the prospect will benefit from meeting with you. Even if it should turn out that the prospect's company and yours are not the best fit for each other, the prospect will have gained insight and heard about new ideas, and may have even found out what the competition is doing. Even if there is no future business relationship, the prospect will have profited from the meeting. That's what you need to convey during the call.

Dismissals

Sales champions know how to listen carefully to differentiate between true objections and mere dismissals.

Dismissals are a prospect's almost automatic reactions. The person has one goal, and one goal only: to get you off the phone and quickly end this interruption of their day. Prospects don't even really think about their response in this second; it doesn't matter to them.

"I'm not interested."

"I'm busy."

"Call me some other time."

The nicer ones might give you a glimmer of hope, with responses like:

"I am interested, please send me some information."

They know from experience that most salespeople don't like confrontation either and will go away quietly, so they are trying to let them down easy and not hurt their feelings. Will they ever look at what you send them? Of course not. They only tried to make you feel less rejected.

Here are the main dismissals you will encounter, including scripts on how to respond:

> *"I am not interested."*
>
> **"Got it. And I don't know if we should be doing business or not, Paul.** *At the same time I did just receive some new market data that shows where your competitors are planning to shift their marketing dollars next year. Does next Monday early afternoon work for a video call?* **I promise I won't waste your time."**

> *"Call me in six months!"*
>
> **"Tom, it's great you guys are planning far in advance. But let me ask you to meet with me anyway next week.** *I'll share with you how Miller Laser Center was able to increase its call volume by 30 percent in the last two months and show you a couple of ideas that I think can help you immediately as well. Does Tuesday later in the morning work for you? Maybe 11 AM? We can meet at your office.* **I promise I won't waste your time."**

> *"Our budget is spent for the remainder of the year."*
>
> **"Oh, it's way too early to talk about money.** *I wanted to first share with you what I see some of your competitors doing really well right now and show you a couple of initial ideas that I*

think can help you. Can you do Monday midafternoon at your office? Maybe 3 PM? **I promise I won't waste your time."**

"Can you email me some information?"
"I certainly can. Let's schedule thirty minutes early next week to review it. *I'll walk you through what I see working in your industry right now and can answer all questions you might have right there. Is Monday at 3 PM good for you for a video call?* **I promise I won't waste your time."**

"I'm busy."
"I figured you would be. And that's exactly why I called. I want to find a time that works better for you *and share with you what I see some of your competitors doing really well right now. How about we get together at your office Tuesday morning instead. 10 AM good for you?* **I promise I won't waste your time."**

"Call my agency!"
"I absolutely will. But let me ask you to meet with me anyway. No one knows your dealership better than you *and I can show you why some of the other Infiniti stores in the area had such a great April. Does Tuesday later in the morning work for a video call? Maybe 11 AM?* **I promise I won't waste your time."**

The beginnings of each of the responses and the last sentences are bold for a reason. Those lines are the ones you should know by heart. They don't change depending on the prospect, and I would argue they also don't change depending on the industry you are in. It's not that hard to learn a few different lines, is it?

In addition to *what* you are saying, it's the delivery that matters. It needs to be completely matter of fact. You must not sound like a desperate salesperson, but instead, like a businessperson who is calling about a business proposition. There should be no stuttering or aggressiveness in your voice, just a confident suggestion.

As you are delivering your first rehearsed line, you have a couple of seconds to think about the middle part of your response (the unbolded parts of the script examples). During this short period, pick your second-best RBR (assuming you used the best one to start off the cold call), then deliver it.

Suggest time, place, and location again ("again," because you most likely already suggested these before you received the dismissal) and finish your response with a line that has worked well for me for almost two decades:

"I promise I won't waste your time."

If you get a second *no* from the prospect, try to follow up with a question. We will explain this a little more when we go over how to react to an objection.

Objections

Objections are different than dismissals. Objections are real reasons prospects are giving you for turning down the meeting, like:

"We just renewed our annual contract with our current vendor. We are happy with them and are not looking to change."

"We are committed to XXX and happy with what we have."

"We are in the middle of executing a huge initiative right now. I can't take on more at this point."

"Radio does not work for us. We have tried it, and it wasn't successful."

"We have done business with your company before and didn't see the return on investment we need."

On the one hand, you can argue objections are easier to handle than dismissals, because prospects give you a (most of the time) truthful rebuttal, which means you at least know their position. On the other hand, the fact that they already have some type of opinion of you, your company, or what you are suggesting—and clearly not a positive one, otherwise they would have granted you the meeting—could mean that it might actually be even harder to get them to change their mind. How can anyone seriously expect to change someone else's mind on anything with a fifteen- to twenty-second response over the phone? It's impossible.

That is why the best strategy to respond to an objection is to deflect instead of fight. Because of thousands of bad salespeople before you, prospects are expecting salespeople to fight back and try to convince them of their opinions and their arguments. You need to take a different approach. Your strategy is to turn what up until this point was a pretty one-sided conversation—you opening the call with your first RBR, then the prospect answering with an objection—into a true dialogue. The best way to do this is by following the five-step objection response framework shown in Figure 12.3:

1	**Recognize and Acknowledge**
2	**Sympathize**
3	**Open-Ended Question**
4	**Position**
5	**Ask for Acceptance**

Figure 12.3: Objection Response Framework

1. You first **recognize** and **acknowledge** that you heard the prospect's objection. While this is partly just good manners, it also gives you a few seconds to think about your follow-up.
2. Next, you **sympathize** with the person, which means you are in a way actually agreeing with the prospect. This comes completely unexpected to prospects. Remember, they are expecting you to do the exact opposite: to disagree with them and fight them over whatever they had said. What this does psychologically is to force prospects to pay a little more attention. Your unexpected response just made them lean in a little bit. And that is your chance.
3. At this moment, you have to follow up with an **open-ended question** that gets prospects to talk, which is exactly what you want. You want them to give you as much information as possible.
4. Based on what prospects are telling you now, your next move is to **position** yourself and your company in a way that makes it

intriguing enough for prospects to agree to meet with you face to face. Many times, you will do this by using one of your backup RBRs.

5. Now, keep your eyes on the prize—the face-to-face meeting—and **ask for acceptance** of your positioning argument and meeting request.

If, during this dialogue with the prospect, you run into a second or even third objection, revert back to the beginning of the objection response framework and start over: recognize and acknowledge, sympathize, ask an open-ended question, position, and ask for acceptance and a meeting.

CASE STUDY:
REBECCA GYMS OBJECTION RESPONSE

You were finally able to get CMO Tracy Ranner on the phone. You opened with the In-Segment Success Story RBR cold-call script from chapter eight, highlighting NYC Media's work with Y7 Studio in New York, and asked to schedule a video call for next week.

Unfortunately—but not unexpectedly—Tracy responded like this:

"We will really be relying on PR efforts during the launch, and not on traditional media. There is really no need for a meeting at this point."

Using the five-step objection response framework, you try to turn the call into a dialogue:

Step I—Recognize and Acknowledge:
"One hundred percent PR focus. Got it."

Step 2—Sympathize:

"And that makes sense. There is no question that word of mouth is a very organic and effective way to stand out from all the advertising messages people are exposed to daily."

Step 3—Question:

"Do you know yet which New York influencers you will be working with?" Tracy tells you she is in conversations with several well-known women in the fitness space who have a substantial number of social media followers.

Step 4—Position:

"Tracy, I think we are able to help you with this strategy and amplify it. Our female on-air personalities here in New York don't just have massive social followings; they are constantly recommending things they like on-air to their listeners. And they do this in a very organic way. Radio is controlled word of mouth. You control the words, you control the number of mentions and impressions. It's a great complement to what you are already planning."

Step 5—Ask for Acceptance:

"Let's schedule a video call for next week to talk a little more about this. I'll have some market segmentation data ready as well, which will be helpful for your launch. Is Monday at 2 PM good for you?"

ENGAGE

13

MEETING THE BUYER FOR THE FIRST TIME

et the fun begin! All the rejection you endured during the Connect phase—the hang-ups, the voicemail messages that were not returned, the seed emails that were deleted—is being rewarded with you meeting the prospect face to face, either in person or on a video call. You earned it! And that's really why you got into sales in the first place, right? Building relationships by being social, maybe even schmoozing them over lunch, and telling prospects about your product or service. Easy work! Well, not so fast.

While most salespeople would pick a first meeting with a buyer over a cold-calling session at the office any day of the week, conducting this meeting effectively is one of the most challenging tasks in the entire sales process, possibly *the* most challenging. To stick with our tennis analogy from earlier, you can look at it as the Wimbledon of all sales calls. A win is difficult to pull off.

Many studies over the years have tried to determine if sales success is correlated more with strong performance during the first meeting with a prospect or during the later proposal meeting, when you actually present your customized solution and try to finalize the deal. It's also a question I ask in sales trainings all the time: Which of the two meetings is more important?

The results are always the same. Sales rookies think success is all tied to their proposal presentation and how they did during the closing phase. Sales aces know better, and the research proves it. Success is determined more by how effective they were in conducting the first meeting with the prospect. It might still take several more meetings with prospects and more time until deals close, but a job well done in this first face-to-face interaction with the buyer is the biggest differentiator of all.

This elevated importance of the first meeting with a buyer is also the reason sales managers of high-performing sales teams prefer to attend first meetings over proposal meetings. That can be a little counterintuitive. Isn't the sales manager supposed to come in toward the end of the sales process and try to help close the deal? The exact opposite is the case. Effective sales managers know that the first meeting takes more finesse, and that their experience is needed more there. Then they stay with the deal through the entire sales process, including the proposal meeting.

AN EFFECTIVE FIRST MEETING TAKES SKILL

Effective salespeople know that an effective first meeting with a buyer needs to accomplish a long list of things, including:

- putting buyers at ease with you and ill at ease with their status quo
- provoking their thinking and opening them up to new possibilities
- building rapport with buyers and determining their personality/ style
- uncovering challenges buyers face and needs they have
- determining if your potential solutions would be a good fit for what buyers need
- uncovering obstacles to buyers making a change and becoming customers
- ensuring buyers see *your company* as a viable future partner
- ensuring buyers see *you* as a viable future partner
- helping buyers understand the process of doing business with you
- gaining a clearer picture on timing and decision-making processes

• walking away with a clearly defined assignment and next step

Easy? Not at all. Unfortunately, much like what you experienced during the initial outreach phase, the cards are also stacked against you when it comes to the first prospect meeting. And again, you can thank all the bad salespeople who were there before you for it. Most buyers keep their guard up and approach the first meeting with a salesperson they have not previously met with caution:

"Another one of these sales guys who will give me a capabilities presentation and claim they are number one."

"When does the dog and pony show start?"

"How long is this going to take?"

"When is he telling me he wants to find out more about my needs?"

"Just another salesperson I have to educate on my business and industry."

"When are they trying to close me?"

"Even if I like what I am hearing, I just don't have the time to make a change right now."

"Success is never guaranteed anyway, and what a pain in the butt it would be to get the others on the team on board."

"I can't even remember why I agreed to the meeting. I have so many other things to get done."

No wonder most sales managers confirm what I have observed for many years: fewer than half of all scheduled first meetings with buyers result in a second meeting. Yes, that also has to do with lack of lead quality. But the fact remains that the majority of first meetings are not successful.

FIRST-MEETING OBJECTIVE

The primary goal of a first meeting is for you to walk away with a clearly defined assignment and next step. Similar to how you measured the effectiveness of a cold-calling session by the number of face-to-face meetings you were able to schedule, measure first-meeting success by the absolute number of assignments you are receiving and the number of assignments as a percentage of all first meetings.

If you want to hold yourself to an even higher standard, measure the quality of your first meeting with prospects by asking yourself: Would prospects be willing to pay you simply for the meeting itself, even if it doesn't result in any further action? Would they pay you because you shared information they didn't have access to or were not aware of? Would they pay you because the quality of your questions led them to conclusions they wouldn't have drawn without your prompting? Would they pay you because the time with you was worth theirs?

While these questions aren't realistic in most real-life sales scenarios, it's important to at least approach first meetings with that mindset. But keep in mind that this is exactly what's happening when you go see a doctor for the first time for an examination. You get charged!

FIRST MEETINGS HAVE EVOLVED OVER TIME

Before the advent of the consultative sales approach, salespeople tried to make the sale in the first meeting with the buyer. They typically brought a lot of information about their company as well as generic "packages," like the infamous "Summer Sizzler," to the meeting, and tried to close the deal on the spot. If that resulted in anything, it was solutions that worked for the vendor more than the prospect.

The consultative sales approach brought a more prospect-focused approach and an emphasis on building a personal relationship with the buyer. It also became popular to ask questions to find out more about the company and its challenges. I vividly remember a sales trainer advising me around 2003 to "bring nothing but a blank piece of paper and a pen and take a lot of notes." Maybe salespeople left a generic brochure or media kit behind on their way out. In contrast to earlier practices, they would then return for a follow-up meeting to impress the prospect with a more customized campaign and try to close the deal.

Conventional wisdom has long held that selling is all about this type of "client needs analysis" and that relationships are the underpinning of most sales success. Yet, over the last ten years, this relationship-based sales approach has become less effective. This doesn't mean that relationships have become less important, far from it. But as Neil Rackham writes in the foreword of *The Challenger Sale*, it seems increasingly that "the customer relationship is the *result* and not the *cause* of successful selling. It is a reward that the salesperson earns by creating value for the prospect." In other words, salespeople earn the right to deep client relationships by providing clients with new, very specific and customized insights, and by helping them think differently.

This is why the terms "discovery meeting" or "client needs analysis," which are often used to describe the first meeting with a prospect, are a little misleading. As you have just read, the first meeting is so much more than "discovering" and "analyzing needs." And as a result, you will find the terms "initial meeting" and "first meeting" used more often in newer sales literature. This book will use the label "first meeting."

STAY IN CONTROL OF THE MEETING

Many years ago, I scheduled a meeting with a brand manager at Toys "R" Us, then a very successful company with big advertising dollars. It was an important meeting, a great opportunity. I had done a lot of research leading up to it and felt prepared. Yet Toys "R" Us, in its corporate office, had its conference rooms named after countries and states, and my meeting was scheduled in the "Alaska" meeting room. Not a good omen! I even remember thinking that I would have preferred the Hawaii room to the potentially icy atmosphere in Alaska.

The buyer had only agreed to a thirty-minute meeting, and, on top of that, arrived ten minutes late. Before I could even begin to go over what I wanted to accomplish in the meeting, the buyer had already cut me off, asking—in a very short and gruff way—"I've only got twenty minutes max. What have you got for me?" And just like that, I froze and threw my entire well-thought-out plan for the meeting overboard and, pretty incoherently, went right into presenting our company and our assets.

It all went downhill from there. The meeting was a complete disaster. And needless to say, there was never a second one.

It was a good lesson, though, one that I have shared with many salespeople over the course of the years. The lesson: you, the salesperson, need to control the first meeting from beginning to end. You, not the buyer. That doesn't mean you should be doing all the talking. In fact, it's quite the opposite actually. We will get to that. But you have to own the process from the moment you shake the buyer's hand to when you say goodbye. You are not just going on a sales call, you are conducting it.

FIRST-MEETING PREPARATION

To accomplish this effectively, you have to do two things before you meet with the prospect face to face. You have to do research and prep work in advance, and you have to plan the meeting and think through the cadence of topics to discuss.

You have already done most of the research legwork during the prospecting phase. As a result, you already know about the company's social media activities, and you have visited its website, canvassed their executive team, and looked at their offers and their positioning. If you were smart, you captured a lot of this data in your CRM. Now, of course, is the time when you have to try to go deeper and find out as much about the company as you can. Look at its most recent press releases, search for recent interviews of senior executives, or speak with colleagues who might know more about the prospect. Read its mission statement and shareholder letter. Sample its product or service and download their app, and maybe even walk into one of the prospect's locations if it is a retailer.

Check out LinkedIn and spend a few minutes reading about your buyer's career. Has the person been with the company for a long time or were they recently hired? Can you draw any conclusions about the buyer's personality based on the different professional roles the person has had? Are they associated with any charities that could make for a good talking point?

The benefit of specializing on a vertical is that you will already understand the terminology used in a specific industry. You will also already be aware of changes in consumer behavior and research studies that are relevant. If you are not, you will have to spend additional time learning about these potential insights. Since one of our strategies to impress the buyer during the first meeting is to lead with insights, this is a crucial step you certainly shouldn't skip.

Once you feel you have uncovered enough information to make the meeting a productive conversation, you need to think through each element of the call.

How are you planning to introduce your process? Which insights can you use to set up an effective question? How can you build a connection between your company and the buyer's? Even more trivial things, like your small-talk topic to break the ice at the beginning of the meeting, need to be considered. You've got to have a plan! Winging it doesn't work anymore, if it ever did. Buyers have higher expectations than ever. There is an old saying in sales that is absolutely still relevant: if you don't have a plan, stay in the car.

One of my go-to questions when accompanying a salesperson to a first meeting with a prospect is *"what's our plan for the meeting?"* You'll notice right away who has a plan and who doesn't. Sales champions will answer with an almost minute-by-minute description of how they are visualizing the meeting and go over insights and questions they have prepared.

Yes, this all sounds like a lot of prep work. And it is. But trust me, buyers can feel the difference when they are approached with purpose by a sales ace. They want to deal with people who have done their homework and take control of things.

THE IMPORTANCE OF FIRST IMPRESSIONS

The first meeting is typically the first time you will be face to face with the buyer, either in person or by video chat. That means you want to make a good first impression, as with any relationship. First impressions are fundamental drivers of our relationships. They are our initial condition for analyzing another human being. Researchers have long asserted that people make up their minds about people they meet for the first time within two minutes. As it turns out, this might even be an underestimate. Malcolm Gladwell writes in *Blink: The Power of Thinking Without Thinking*, that these decisions may occur much faster—instantaneously, or in no more than two seconds. In other words, you have no room for error and need to be on top of your game from the moment you shake the buyer's hand or appear on video.

Professor Frank Bernieri of Oregon State University, drawing on several research studies, offers two things to consider if you want to make a good first impression:

First, be open. "There's a behavioral principle known as the expressivity halo—people who communicate in an expressive, animated fashion tend to be liked more than difficult-to-read people," says Bernieri. "Because we're more confident in our reading of them, they're less of a threat." I know many hugely successful salespeople who are introverts. When they are in front of their prospects or clients, though—especially for the first time—you would never know. They are "on." It's a little bit like watching actors morph into a role. A strong handshake, good eye contact, and a confident smile are part of that role.

Second, make the effort to discover things you have in common. Books you have read, films you have seen, mutual friends, or even enemies are things that can create a powerful bond. "It's called the similarity attraction hypothesis," says Bernieri. "It's powerful because it's a cognitive processing phenomenon—a reflex, not an analytical skill."

Sales champions can adapt with a chameleon's speed and skill to buyers' various behavioral styles. Much like in sports, where successful coaches have to alter their game plan as they face different teams, successful salespeople do the same with different buyers they are meeting with for the first time.

If you bring your sales manager to the meeting, don't just introduce her as "my manager," but explain why you decided to bring her along. *"Jane has more than twenty years' experience working with companies in your industry and just oversaw the execution of a project for a client who seems to be in a very comparable situation as you. I think she will be able to add value today, and that's why I brought her along."*

FIRST-MEETING SEATING ARRANGEMENTS

Seating arrangements will vary depending on the buyer's type of business. There is certainly a difference if you are meeting in the buyer's actual office or in a conference room. Ideally, you know in advance what type of setting you will be walking into. Again, that's another reason why it pays to establish a good relationship with gatekeepers.

For example: if you meet in the buyer's office, with the buyer sitting behind the desk and you facing the buyer from the other side of the desk (a common scenario in many small- to medium-sized business meetings), showing a PowerPoint deck built for the big screen of a conference room will most likely not be very effective. While this sounds trivial, it's important to think these things through in advance.

Figure 13.1 shows a few examples of conference room settings:

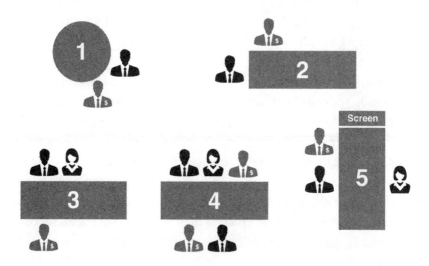

Figure 13.1: Five Different First-Meeting Seating Scenarios ($ = Salesperson)

A first meeting with a new prospect is not some diplomatic mission, so don't feel obligated to automatically sit across from your prospect, on the opposite side of the conference room table. You are not negotiating a nuclear arms treaty with Russia. If you sit on the opposite side, it will give the meeting a certain "negotiating" atmosphere, when all you want to do at this point is have a business conversation with the buyer. It's already hard enough to build rapport with a person you have never met before—no need to create an additional divide.

If you are sitting at a round table (Scenario 1 in Figure 13.1), try to sit next to the buyer and work from one handout instead of two separate ones. If it's a longer rectangular table, which is typical for many conference and boardrooms, and you are meeting with one person (Scenario 2), try to sit at a ninety-degree angle, with either the prospect or you sitting at the head of the table. If there are more than two people in the meeting, the seating arrangements change slightly (Scenarios 3 and 4), but a good guiding principle is to mix up salespeople and buyers as much as possible, instead of one company team sitting on one side of the conference table and the other team across from it. If you are planning to project some of your information on a large TV screen in a conference room (Scenario 5), it definitely helps if you are the one sitting closest to the screen. That way buyers don't have to consistently turn between the screen and you.

FIRST MEETING AS A VIDEO CALL

The number of first-time face-to-face meetings that are conducted over video call has increased exponentially since COVID-19 arrived on our shores. It is important to follow best practices for virtual first meetings to maximize their effectiveness:

- Let the prospect know in advance the meeting will be a video call and not a phone call, for example by including it in your confirmation email the day before, and in the subject line of your meeting invite.
- Make sure your computer volume is turned up.
- Practice sharing your screen, video, and files before the meeting. But only share your screen and presentation when it helps to make your point. The better the participants can see each other, the more

conversational the video meeting will be. It is absolutely okay to share your screen for a couple of minutes, un-share, then share again at a different point in the meeting.

- Dress like you would if you were meeting the prospect in person.
- Be aware of your background. I personally don't like blurred backgrounds. Instead, I like to make my background interesting in order to spark a conversation. At the time of writing, the main items buyers can see behind me on a video call are a Pac-Man arcade console, several tennis rackets, a Tottenham Hotspur soccer ball from 1953, and a picture of the New York Mets. Rarely does a prospect not comment on at least one of these things.
- Sit in a well-lit location, ideally with a window or lamp in front of you, not behind you.
- Limit distractions. For example, turn off your computer notifications, silence your cell phone, and put a "Do Not Disturb" sign outside your closed door.
- Act as if you are conducting the meeting in person. Look straight into the camera instead of at your screen to establish good eye contact. Even more than in a typical in-person setting, acknowledge that you understand what the buyer is saying by clearly nodding or smiling.
- Ask buyers to turn on their cameras. If you are on video, most people will get the hint even without asking. But if necessary, don't be shy about inquiring if they have video capabilities. It's called a face-to-face meeting for a reason.

YOU ARE SELLING DURING THE FIRST MEETING

In most B2B sales situations (at least the ones we are focusing on in this book), the actual product, service, or solution will not be sold in the first meeting. But don't believe for a second you are not selling during this first meeting with a buyer. You absolutely must be selling in order to move the ball forward.

You accomplish this by making mini-sales along the way. You started doing this in your earlier confirmation email by including a small assignment for the prospect to complete (your first "yes"). In that email, you asked them to read an article, complete a survey, invite someone else within the company, or think about a topic you are planning to discuss. Now you will continue to do that throughout this meeting and beyond. The best first meetings are the ones where both parties walk away with a to-do list to complete before the follow-up meeting. The more you do that, the more engaged the buyer will be throughout the sales process.

You want buyers to believe that, based on the case studies and insights you're sharing, your company is a potential partner for them (another "yes"). Selling them on your process at this stage is much more effective than focusing on your product. What is it like working with your company? What are next steps you can agree upon (the next "yes")? And, of course, you are selling yourself: your experience, your background, your successes, your commitment, your dedication. You want the buyer thinking:

"This person is impressive. Let's see if the concept and ideas she will come back to me with are also good. But I can work with her for sure." Another "yes."

These mini-sales during the first meeting add up and establish your credibility.

The first meeting is also the right time to sell your buyer on the "neighborhood." Yes, you read that right, the *neighborhood*. Many industries can learn from real estate sales. If you have ever bought a house, you know that before a good real estate agent actually shows you a listed home, he first drives you around the neighborhood to make sure he gets your buy-in. Here is the excellent school; look at the wide variety of retailers at the mall; the movie theater has eight auditoriums; a river with a running trail is only three minutes away. You get the idea. Only once you are sold on the neighborhood does the agent give you a tour of the actual house.

Transfer this to a sales situation in—let's say—the radio industry. Would you start describing how great the radio stations you are representing are in the first meeting with the prospect? Would you explain how many listeners they have and that one of the morning shows is number one in the market? No, you wouldn't. Instead you should focus on the power of audio advertising, what type of success companies that have shifted advertising dollars to the audio space are seeing, and how audio complements TV or digital advertising so well. Audio (the neighborhood) first; stations/concepts/solutions (the home) second, in the follow-up meeting.

14

FIRST-MEETING FRAMEWORK

S imilar to our cold call, seed email, voicemail, and objections frameworks, your first meetings with buyers will be more effective if you follow a process. The more you can replicate the same process in meeting after meeting, the more ingrained it will become in your efforts over time, and the more it will allow you to focus instead on the content of the meeting.

A study authorized by the CEB Sales Leadership Council showed that 53 percent of customer loyalty is based on the sales experience itself, not on the product or the company. That means that *how* you sell has more impact than *what* you sell. If you are selling for a company that is maybe less well known, or doesn't necessarily have the best product in the market, this is an even more important fact. Following a structured process in the first meeting with the buyer plays a big role here. As you will notice, we will spend much more time analyzing how this meeting should look than on how to conduct an effective proposal meeting. The reason, as already mentioned, is that many more things can go wrong in first meetings—they are the true differentiators.

Figure 14.1 shows the seven phases of our first-meeting framework, which we will cover in detail in the next few sections and chapters. While

1	**Build Rapport**
2	**"Here Is What I Wanted to Get Done Today"**
3	**Use Power Stories to Build Credibility**
4	**Discover Challenges and Needs**
5	**Teach and Personalize**
6	**Clarify Assignment and Next Steps**
7	**Confirm Assignment**

Figure 14.1: First Prospect Meeting Framework

the length of your first prospect meetings will partly depend on the industry you are working in, forty-five minutes is typically the time you'll need to cover the six steps of the first-meeting framework. The seventh step will be completed after the meeting.

BUILD RAPPORT

The first phase of the first meeting is all about connecting with the buyer on a personal level. This comes naturally to some and takes a little bit more work and preparation for others. Our goal, of course, is to get buyers to open up a little and ideally find some commonalities. You want to have at least one small-talk item in mind that you can fall back on, in case no other topic of conversation arises. That can be a breaking news story, the horrendous traffic on the way over, last night's sports game, or other things. Avoid awkward silences at the beginning of the meeting at all costs. It's like going on a date and not finding anything to talk about. It usually doesn't end well.

Commenting on certain personal items displayed at your buyer's office can be a good conversation starter. But approach it with caution. You have to assume every salesperson your buyer saw in the last three months was doing the exact same thing. It can definitely come across as cheesy and tattoo the word "salesperson" on your forehead if you don't find the right tone here. Yet people do love talking about themselves and their achievements. If someone has a framed golf scorecard hanging on the wall, showcasing a hole in one at Pebble Beach, I'd bring it up. If it's just a picture of his family at the beach, I wouldn't. Use your best judgment here.

I have been working with a very successful salesperson who has been moonlighting as "Jetman" for the New York Jets for many years. One day he sits down in a buyer's office and notices a picture of a young boy at a Jets game. And not just that—the other person in the picture was Jetman. He was looking at a picture of himself with the buyer's son! Of course Jetman commented on it and landed a big new business deal.

Some salespeople usually skip over this small-talk phase too quickly. They might have heard somewhere that small talk is "old school" and that they should just get to business right away. I think that's a mistake. Take the time and build initial rapport as long as you think the prospect wants the small talk to last. It will also help you better determine who you are dealing with. Are you speaking with an extroverted "talker" who is going on about his weekend plans forever, or someone who is "all business" and doesn't want to waste time on any topics but business? Be flexible and adjust, but eventually shift the conversation to what you are trying to accomplish in today's meeting.

"HERE IS WHAT I WANTED TO GET DONE TODAY"

Of all seven phases in the first-meeting framework, this one is the shortest. It takes no more than a minute. It is, in my experience, also among the most important phases. Walking buyers through what you have in mind for the next forty-five minutes doesn't just show them that you are taking control of the meeting; it also sets the tone for what is to come. Many salespeople skip this step, and every time I witness it I see a train wreck in the immediate sales future.

Compared to the many other things a salesperson has to do throughout the sales process, this seems to be an easy task. I never understood why it is not. It might be a mix of not wanting to come across as "scripted" and not having the confidence to take charge of the meeting. Some simply forget to do it, maybe because they were thrown off by an unexpected question the buyer asked them at the beginning of the meeting, similar to what happened to me in the first meeting with the Toys "R" Us buyer. The good news is that if you do this step well, you will stand out from most other salespeople right away, at the start of the client relationship.

An effective setup aligns expectations by doing the following:

- Builds credibility by highlighting your preparation for the meeting
- Shares the agenda of the meeting
- Establishes that you are here to have a conversation, not to give a presentation
- Ensures the prospect knows you brought customized information, insights, and the like to show—just not right away
- Explains your process of working with buyers
- Takes the pressure out of the meeting, since the buyer understands immediately you are not planning to ask for an order today
- Informs the buyer you will be taking notes to make sure that all the information covered in the meeting will be captured
- Lets the buyer know there will be a next step if both parties decide a next step makes sense
- Contracts for time by confirming the buyer is available for the time originally scheduled

The way you set the stage for the first meeting doesn't change much from meeting to meeting. And whenever that's the case in sales, I advocate crafting a well-thought-out script that salespeople can learn once—even by heart—and then use all the time. Just make sure the script fits your style and you can deliver it conversationally. You just finished making small talk with the buyer, so there's no need to suddenly sound completely different. Keep the conversation flow the same.

I have been successfully using the phrase *"Here is what I wanted to get done today"* to transition from the building-rapport phase to the more business-focused conversation for years. Try it out, but use what works best for you. *"This is the way I work"* or *"Here is what I would like to do"* are similar options for openings.

When you set up the first meeting with prospects, you used one or several Relevant Business Reasons to pique their interest. There is no need to feel obligated now to focus on these right away, in the first meeting, for several reasons. First, it is very likely that buyers already forgot what you said or wrote when you reached out. Buyers are busy, and as much as we want to believe that the meeting with us is the highlight of their week, it is not. Second, focusing especially on an idea RBR too quickly will limit your options to sell a comprehensive solution too early. As a result, you might be leaving money on the table. A buyer might become so enamored with one specific idea that they don't pay enough attention to other potential strategies and opportunities. If, after conducting a more thorough analysis of their challenges, your original idea seems the best solution for what the prospect is trying to accomplish, absolutely share it later in the meeting as an idea starter. But don't do so right out of the gate. An RBR is just the tip of the sales spear that gets you the meeting, nothing more. The more you can keep your options open initially, the better.

CASE STUDY:
REBECCA GYMS SCRIPT FOR SHARING THE AGENDA

After some initial small talk with CMO Tracy Ranner, you are transitioning the video call to Phase 2. A script for this transition could look like this:

> *"Tracy, here is what I wanted to get done today. I did as much research as I could on Rebecca Gyms' business and positioning in the West Coast markets you are currently in, and, of course, checked out your website and social media presence. I wasn't*

> *able to actually visit a location since you are not open yet in New York, but I did speak with a friend of mine in LA who is a very happy member and gave me a very good description. I do have a few more questions to better understand your marketing strategy and especially your plans around the launch in New York, though. I brought the Y7 case study I mentioned on the phone as well as a couple of idea starters that I wanted to go over later. Hopefully we both see that there is a fit and that NYC Media can be of help with your campaign. I'd then go back to our creative team, brainstorm with our producers, and talk to some of our female on-air personalities. That's how we'll come up with a customized proposal based on all the parameters you are giving me today. We had planned to meet for forty-five minutes. Are you still good on time? Great! If it's okay with you, I'll take notes so I have all the important info when I work on the campaign back at the office."*

USE POWER STORIES TO BUILD CREDIBILITY

You had engaging small talk with the buyer to begin the meeting, and then differentiated yourself from most other salespeople by sharing your agenda and plan for the meeting. The buyer is not only on the same page as you, but is also impressed by your professionalism so far. At about ten minutes into the meeting, you are on the way to building enough credibility with your buyer to engage in a productive discovery conversation.

Many salespeople at this point jump right into the client needs analysis and start asking questions. I have always felt that to be a little bit too early. To get the prospect to really open up, you need to raise your credibility even further. You accomplish this by giving a 90- to 120-second summary of how you work with your partners.

How do businesses benefit from working with your company and using your products and services? What types of results are clients seeing from your solutions? Which other companies are already working with you? Your short opener needs to be so compelling that it makes the buyer lean in. It needs to be intriguing enough to convince buyers that the rest of the meeting is worth their effort, focus, and time. That's what we call the "power story."

Is "power story" just another term for "elevator speech," "value proposition," or "unique selling proposition"? It shouldn't be. These terms are so overused and quite frankly never really made much sense. Has anyone ever actually asked you about your company in an elevator? More importantly, though, they typically only talk about what a company does, what types of products it offers, and in general mostly brag about how the company is the best, biggest, fastest, and smartest. They are self-centered, not customer-focused. *"We produce . . . ," "We were founded in . . . ," "We have . . . ," "We are . . . ," "We are ranked . . ."* Prospects don't care about these types of scripts.

And it's not even the salespeople that deserve the blame here. It's usually the sales managers who don't put enough emphasis on developing and teaching a concise, customer-focused narrative of how their company works with its partners. If you don't want to wait for your sales manager to come up with a power story for your company, I highly recommend Mike Weinberg's book *New Sales. Simplified*, which gives the reader detailed instructions on how to develop an effective power statement from scratch.

What buyers care about is how you and your company can help them solve their challenges. The problem, of course, is that you don't know at this point how much the buyer already knows about your company and what you actually do. And maybe that's why some salespeople feel obligated to launch into their sales braggadocio right away. Instead, let's ask the buyer.

"How familiar are you with us?"

Especially in industries like media, where you may be meeting with a potential future client as well as a potential current listener, reader, viewer, or fan of your brands and shows, this can shift the dynamic of the meeting dramatically. Answers like *"I am using your app every day"* or *"I am a huge fan of your morning show. I listen every day in my car on the way to work"* put a little more wind in your sales sails. On the flip side, a response like *"I don't have a car and haven't listened to radio in years"* means you have a little more of an uphill battle ahead. This is important information to have early in your conversation.

Successful sales forces know their power stories. They study them, practice them, and use them. Sometimes they use the entire power story narrative, and sometimes just snippets of it. They use them in seed emails, they use them to address objections, they use them at networking events when they introduce themselves and describe what they do professionally. You can tell sales teams are unfocused if you ask all twenty salespeople on a team how they describe the company to prospects in ninety seconds and get twenty different answers. A great, client-focused power story can function as a unifying theme that instills confidence into a sales force. When salespeople buy into the company's sales story, it creates a sense of pride that is infectious, both with other team members and with customers.

A compelling power story consists of three elements:

- An attention-grabbing opening: In a couple of short sentences, you introduce the company and its mission. If buyers are not familiar with your company at all, make sure you provide enough context for them to understand what type of business and industry you are in.
- A list of customer challenges and how your company solves them: You immediately turn to several (usually three to five) problems your customers are facing and, without any bragging, state why your customers turn to you for help.
- Clients your company is working with: You raise your credibility further by mentioning a few businesses with high name recognition that show prospects they would be in good company. Choose the client names carefully depending on the industry your prospect is in. The more relevant and the closer they are to what your prospect is doing, the better.

Other than swapping out client names, can power stories change depending on which prospect you are speaking with? They absolutely can, although you certainly don't want to put yourself in a position of having to learn a new power story every time you meet a new buyer. That would be unrealistic and too time consuming. Your best bet is to focus on the items in a power story that are most relevant to a particular prospect and its situation, and to leave out the ones that are not.

For power stories to be delivered most effectively, they need to be incorporated into the conversation you are already having with the buyer. You aren't using PowerPoint slides, printouts, or brochures. It is just you looking the buyer in the eye and delivering your story, not in a "salesy" tone, but very much matter of fact. You're one businessperson telling another how your company is solving problems for its partners.

CASE STUDY:
NYC MEDIA POWER STORY FOR
REBECCA GYMS

A power story for a local media company like NYC Media, to be used in a first meeting with Rebecca Gyms CMO Tracy Ranner, could sound like this:

> *"NYC Media is the only locally-operated media company in New York that focuses on local magazines, local radio stations, and local websites. Our mission is to entertain and inform diverse and opinionated New Yorkers.*
> *Marketers turn to us . . .*
>
> * *When they need someone to help them with their PR and sound strategy in an age when music and audio are becoming more and more important to consumers and editorial content is offering a better way to stand out from the competition.*
> * *When they realize that influencers can help them make their message more believable and memorable with consumers that are increasingly distracted.*

- *Because as a New York–based and –operated company we understand the New York consumer better than anyone and can give our partners access to many different communities.*
- *Because trust is at the top of every marketer's mind. And magazines and radio are the most trusted media of all.*
- *When they are looking for a cross-platform approach that maximizes return on investment.*

Y7 Studio and Puma, for example, faced several of these challenges when they started working with us, and have been seeing excellent results. New York Sports Club and Revlon are as well."

Then, transition to the next phase of the first meeting:

"I will show you some of the learnings from their campaigns later, but let me ask you about your New York launch first."

DISCOVER CHALLENGES AND NEEDS

In terms of percentage of time each of the phases takes up, finding out more details about the company, its strategy, competition, and current partners, as well as the buyers themselves, is at the top of the list. More selling can be done by asking great questions than by projecting a Power-Point presentation on a screen. This is the phase of the first meeting that is indeed a "client needs analysis" and is so important that we will cover it in chapters fifteen and sixteen in more detail.

TEACH AND PERSONALIZE

It's finally time to go over the information you put together for the buyer leading up the meeting. You can look at this phase as reverse discovery. Now it's time for the buyer to find out more about your company and product. If you think this is about going over a generic brochure or polished presentation, though, you are very much mistaken. You don't want to lose your conversational style throughout the meeting. Instead, you will teach and impress by discussing insights and research about the prospect's consumers, competitors, and industry. You will also walk buyers through case studies that address challenges similar to theirs.

We will go into more detail on which material is the most effective to show a buyer in chapters seventeen and eighteen.

CLARIFY ASSIGNMENT AND NEXT STEPS

Millions of sales hours have been wasted by overly optimistic salespeople who thought they had received an assignment from a buyer and spent a week putting together a kick-ass proposal, only to find out during the proposal meeting that the buyer doesn't have anywhere near the budget you are requesting, or was under a very different impression about which one of their challenges you would be trying to solve.

Asking for and clarifying assignments and next steps is what separates sales champions from sales rookies. It is a skill that many salespeople struggle with. We will introduce a step-by-step script that can be used as a blueprint for this phase of the first meeting in chapter nineteen.

CONFIRM AND SUMMARIZE ASSIGNMENT

The last step in the first-meeting framework doesn't actually happen during the meeting, but after the meeting with the buyer, when you confirm your assignment in writing in a follow-up email. To make the greatest impact and set yourself apart from other salespeople, you need to complete this the day of the meeting, not two or three days later. Get the email out when the information covered in the meeting is still fresh, on both your and the buyer's side. In it, you'll summarize the main points discussed in the meeting. You'll include information you gathered from the prospect that is important to developing the customized solution, and what the tailored proposal you will develop will try to accomplish. You'll also spell out a budget range to make sure both parties are on the same page.

We will review what you need to include in this confirmation email in chapter twenty.

LET THE BUYER TALK

You can see why the first meeting with a prospect is far from easy. You need to cover many different elements, all of it in a conversational style, in a no-pressure atmosphere you create that puts the buyer at ease and allows for an honest dialogue, yet moves the ball forward through mutual agreement on clearly defined next steps. In case you are wondering what the overall talk ratio between you and the prospect should be during the first meeting, remember that we are trying to have a conversation between businesspeople. And a good conversation is typically an engaging back and forth between two interested parties. A first meeting feels "right" if the buyer talks for about two-thirds of the meeting and the salesperson for the other third. That means you will walk away with a lot of useful information and that you had enough time to cover material of interest to the buyer.

DISCOVER

15

NOBODY HAS EVER LISTENED THEMSELVES OUT OF A SALE

t's more important to understand than to convince. Prospects buy because they feel the salesperson understands their problems. It's what Ori from Allegro Piano in the story at the beginning of the book practices, and it's something sales champions know: great questions make the difference and set up a salesperson for success. That, of course, runs counter to what most people think of as "selling." It's not the salesperson talking; it's the salesperson getting the buyer to talk.

Learning to ask effective questions takes time, and crafting great questions takes preparation. I am always stunned when salespeople don't feel the need to consider in advance the questions they are planning to ask in a first buyer meeting. Only very few actually write them down and practice them before the meeting. And even fewer are confident enough to take out their notebook with the prepared questions in front of the prospect. Meanwhile, prospects absolutely respect this. Try it!

Yet even the best questions won't get you far if you don't learn how to become a good listener. When you speak, you just repeat what you already know. When you listen, you actually learn something. Unfortunately, when you bring up the topic of effective listening in sales meetings, it's not uncommon for many participants to tune out and check their emails. How hard can listening be? In fact, it's much easier said than done, probably because most people can *think* much faster than the average person *talks*, which allows the mind to wander. Listening requires determination and concentration. To determine the prospect's challenges that you can help address and solve, you need to hear what the prospect is saying and uncover the information you need.

FAKE LISTENING

There is an important difference between fake and effective listening. Fake listening is listening with a closed mind. You are busy forming the next question in your mind, while the prospect is still answering the last one. You are predisposed to your own opinion and focused on what you want to accomplish, so you filter out things you don't want to hear and only hear things you do. And you only listen long enough to figure out if the prospect's view conforms with your own. Fake listening is a mindset where you're just "checking off a box" before you move on to talk about what your company has to offer. It's better than not uncovering any information from buyers, of course, but fake listening also ensures you will miss important challenges they are facing, and with those, sales opportunities.

A few years ago a salesperson told me she had gotten into the habit of recording first meetings on her iPhone, with permission of her prospects. I cannot recommend it. It's almost an excuse not to listen intently during the actual meeting, and in most situations has a detrimental effect on how open buyers will be with their answers. There is a reason why reporters get the best scoops off the record, and not on.

EFFECTIVE LISTENING

Effective listening, on the other hand, is when you pay attention to every word and look for nonverbal clues to add context to the answer. Effective listening means clarifying answers, paraphrasing to show that you understood what was said, taking notes, and asking follow-up questions. You are "leaning in" mentally and physically to capture and understand everything that is being said. It means you are approaching what you are hearing without prejudice and are not jumping to conclusions too early, before you hear the entire situation. Effective listening means that there will sometimes be short silences while you are processing the information you are receiving, and that's appropriate. The word "listen" contains the same letters as the word "silent," and when we are silent, we obtain greater insights.

We not only "learn" when we listen, we also "earn" when we listen, as we are provided clues on how to present our assets and ideas more effectively in the next phase of this first meeting. And, almost as a side effect, effective listening also conveys respect and helps us gain the buyer's trust. When you really care about listening intently instead of just treating the conversation as another opportunity to make a sale, buyers can sense it. One of the greatest strengths of sales champions is their curiosity. It's a personality trait that helps them dig deeper for answers, which means they are able to get buyers to let down their guard more. As a result, buyers go beyond mere facts and give them more stories and behind-the-scenes information, all of which has the important side effect of buyers becoming emotionally involved in the sales process.

Broadcast sales legend Bob McCurdy shared the following tips on effective listening:

- Avoid being so focused on what you are going to say that you miss what is being said. When concentrating on what you are going to say, you are paying attention to yourself, not the person speaking.

- Listen with empathy. By intently focusing on the speaker, it is easier to see things from their point of view. Seek to understand.
- Slow it down. Take a breath before responding. Even though it might not be the case, it does comes across as more thoughtful.
- Write down any questions you might have prior to the meeting. This frees you up to listen. You can't both listen and figure out what to say next. If you're like most people, you jump back and forth between the two, missing half of what the prospect is saying, which could include information relevant to your business case.
- Get in the habit of repeating back at least some of what you have heard before launching into a response.

16

JUDGE A PERSON BY THEIR QUESTIONS RATHER THAN THEIR ANSWERS

François-Marie Arouet, more famous under the pen name Voltaire, was aware of the power of great questions even as early as the eighteenth century. What he might not have known or cared about back then is a fact that is essential to everyone in a twenty-first-century sales profession: the fastest way to set yourself apart from your competition and add value is through intelligent questions.

At some point growing up, we have all been told that "there are no stupid questions." While that might be true in many situations outside sales, it is certainly the wrong advice for a first meeting with a buyer. Your questions need to be well thought out and have substance. The last thing you want is for buyers to feel they are helping a high school student with a term paper rather than talking shop with a professional colleague with lots of business savvy. Every question you ask will either enhance or detract from your credibility.

With all the data available on the internet, asking intelligent questions has become more important than ever. Buyers simply don't have the time or patience to answer questions you easily could have answered yourself by spending ten minutes on their website or searching Google. There is a big difference between a question like *"How many retail locations do you have?"* and *"My research shows that you currently have seven locations in the Bronx, five in Queens, and that you just broke ground to build a new flagship store in Brooklyn. Any plans for additional new locations this year?"*

Your best questions will be informed by insights: *"We are seeing this, does that apply here as well?"* The more your questions are driven by insights, the more knowledgeable you will come across and the more thought your buyers will put into their responses.

As in so many areas, your category expertise will be very beneficial here. Given your experience with other clients in the same industry and your research, you can lead with hypotheses of prospects' needs and challenges. Prospects like this because it feels more like a "get" than a "give." They get your informed perspective rather than them having to educate you on the basics of their business. Correct use of terminology and jargon specific to their industry also plays an important role here.

Great discovery questions have the power to:

- get the wheels turning inside the buyer's head
- channel the buyer's attention on what matters
- make the buyer "glad you asked"
- provoke reflection and thought
- generate curiosity and stimulate interest in what's possible
- demonstrate your knowledge and preparation
- make you look good—more interesting, imaginative, creative, and knowledgeable than other salespeople
- generate forward sales momentum

ASK LIKE COLUMBO

When I grew up in Austria in the '70s and '80s, we only had two broadcast TV channels to choose from. Every weeknight at 6:30 PM we had the
choice between the local news on one channel and an American TV show
like *Knight Rider, Hart to Hart, Magnum, P.I.,* or *The Waltons* on the other.
That, of course, was the channel that was on in the Weiss household.

One of my favorite shows was *Columbo,* a program about Lieutenant
Columbo, a homicide detective with the Los Angeles Police Department.
I always loved how Columbo used his deferential and absent-minded per-
sona to lull criminal suspects into a false sense of security by asking them
questions in a very nonthreatening manner, using a relaxed, conversational style, without letting them know that they were suspects.

Salespeople can learn a lot from Columbo, whose conversations with
suspects never felt like interrogations. We already covered earlier how
important it is to conduct a first meeting with a buyer as a productive
dialogue between two businesspeople as opposed to one person presenting
to or interviewing the other. Since this chapter is about great questioning
techniques, it bears repeating here. When sales champions work with a
prospect, a fly on the wall could not tell which of the two people is the
salesperson and which one is the buyer.

Notice what Columbo does when he uncovers a discrepancy. He follows up the previous question by digging deeper, asking clarifying questions, and probing until he gets to the bottom of things. An effective needs
analysis does the same thing. You uncover a specific business challenge
and then zero in on it to get beneath the surface and find the real causes
associated with it. What are the ramifications of this problem area for
the company? Other departments? The future? What else? Keep probing;
make it "hurt" a little. Ask them to elaborate. A great way to do this is to
say, *"Tell me more about that."* Leo Burnett, who was responsible for creating some of the twentieth century's most well-known advertising characters and campaigns, including Tony the Tiger and the Marlboro Man,
said, "There is an inherent drama in every product or business. Our No. 1
job is to dig for it and capitalize on it."

OPEN-ENDED AND CLOSED-ENDED QUESTIONS

Start wide, by asking open-ended questions, and then use closed-ended questions to narrow down and clarify.

Open-ended questions will uncover the most information. They are questions that cannot be answered with *yes* or *no*. Rather, they get the prospect talking by starting with *what*, *why*, *where*, *how*, *who*, or *when*.

Closed-ended questions, on the other hand, prompt short *yes* or *no* answers. They are not inherently bad, even if some sales books would like to make you believe that. While you want most of your questions to be open ended, you should absolutely feel comfortable using closed-ended clarifying questions that check your understanding. Closed-ended questions work when they are used to nail down specific information like, *"Your fiscal year starts in July?"*

If a business challenge you uncover wakes the urge to start pitching, please resist. Average salespeople sometimes see an immediate opportunity once buyers start sharing real issues that their company or department has been struggling with. This is not the time to lean in and offer up a solution. Rather, keep asking to get to the root cause of the issue.

Once you have uncovered several business challenges and desired business results, prioritize them together with the prospect and wind your way toward finding the ones you will be focusing on when you develop your solution.

DISCOVERY QUESTIONS FRAMEWORK

Most probing questions can be grouped into one of six categories, shown in Figure 16.1. While a framework is helpful in many aspects here, keep the conversation as flexible as possible. Don't be too rigid, unwilling to break from your standard script or prepared questions. Allow prospects to take the conversation into their areas of interest and don't restrict the topics to yours.

Figure 16.1: Discovery Questions Framework

Try to cover all questions you have in one category at once, and when you feel you have all the information you need, move on to the next category. Too much jumping back and forth between topics just means you are running the risk of not being able to get beneath the surface and of walking away with mostly superficial answers.

It is also important to ask one question at a time. If you combine two or three topics in one question, you run the risk that your prospect only addresses one of them. There is also no need to ask millions of questions. Focus on the essentials, find the pain points, and work your way to assignments from there.

In the following pages, we will provide examples for effective open-ended questions for each of the six question categories. Keep in mind, though, that the more customized each question can be for each sales situation, the better. Our examples have to be more generic, but they should still be helpful in your quest to formulate tailored questions for specific prospect situations.

Personal Questions

Getting to know buyers on a personal level and finding out more about them and their role within their organization is important.

Asking a question like *"How long have you been with the company?"* can open the door to a deeper conversation about whether they previously had another role in the organization, and to learn more about their background. Even more effective would be to connect on LinkedIn first and make the question even more specific: *"I saw that you joined the company last year from (name of previous employer). What convinced you to make the move?"*

As you can see in Figure 16.1, personal questions can be used at any time in the first meeting with buyers. It really depends on what impression you have of the buyer's personality after the first few minutes of the meeting. If you feel you have established enough rapport, feel free to use personal questions as warm-ups for the other questions at the beginning of the discovery phase. If your buyer comes across as "all business," you may want to wait a little longer and ask them later in the meeting. I once was with a young account executive whose first question to the buyer was something along the lines of, *"What are your personal goals?"* The buyer's response— *"None of your business"*—certainly stung.

Examples of personal questions are:

- *"With all the different dynamics in the marketplace, how has your role changed over the last few years?"*
- *"People in your position usually are focused on ___. What are your main responsibilities?"*
- *"How closely are you personally working with the procurement department?"*
- *"What service are you personally using? (e.g., What do you like to listen to?)"*
- *"What made you take this new job?"*
- *"How are you being evaluated? How can I make you look good to your bosses?"*

Competitive Advantage Questions

All successful companies have some type of unique selling proposition, which helps them to differentiate and position themselves in the marketplace.

Great questions during this phase really get buyers talking because many answers will go to the core of what they think about every day. It's what keeps them up at night and is the lifeblood of their business. It's also what makes their company successful or, if things are not going well, points toward the main reasons they are not hitting their goals. This is where you discuss strategy and plans.

It is particularly essential that you do your research in advance for this category of questions. The times you can ask a prospect what the company's tagline is are long gone.

Examples here are:

- *"What sets you apart from the competition? What makes your business unique?"*
- *"If I spoke to several of your customers, what would they say keeps them coming back?"*
- *"In one sentence, what does your business stand for? What's the one word that comes to your customers' minds when they think about your company?"*
- *"What is your staff struggling with the most right now?"*
- *"What's the biggest misconception about your business that you feel needs to be addressed?"*
- *"Where is your product or business in its life cycle?"*
- *"Are there any potential charity tie-ins we should consider?"*
- *"What is your biggest challenge right now, business and/or marketing-wise?"*
- *"What are your plans in regard to . . . ?"*
- *"Do you have any programs set up specifically for diversity initiatives?"*

Consumer Questions

Understanding the company's current customers and potential future customers is essential to coming up with an effective customized solution. If available, look at third-party research in advance of the meeting to help you guide your questions. If you work in the media industry, Nielsen

Scarborough or Mediamark Research and Intelligence (MRI) are good sources of this data. You want to analyze demographic profiles and psychographic data of the prospect's core consumers.

What are typical buying behaviors? Who in the family makes the buying decisions for their products or services? What customer segments are they currently not seeing success in?

Sometimes, buyers will respond to questions about their customer base with, *"I am trying to reach everyone."* Very, very few businesses and brands successfully target all demographic and psychographic consumer segments. And clearly, an answer like this is not enough for you to build an effective solution. You have to dig deeper: *"I understand. Roughly, what do you think the percentage of twenty- to forty-year-olds of your total customer base is?"* Then narrow it down further from there.

Examples of consumer questions are:

- *"Who do you consider the ideal customer in terms of age, gender, and other demographics?"*
- *"Do you have different target customers for different products?"*
- *"What's your primary service area in terms of geography? Where do your customers come from?"*
- *"Are there any customer segments you want to pursue more aggressively?"*
- *"Tell me about the customer journey all the way until they purchase your product."*
- *"What is the most common question a shopper will ask first?"*
- *"In what ways have customer expectations changed in the last couple of years?"*
- *"Do most customers tend to know what they want, or are more of them seeking help and information?"*

Competition Questions

Next, find out more information about the company's competitors. How do they position themselves in the market? What type of marketing are they doing? What are their core strategies? Who is the market leader and—if available—what do market shares of the top three competitors look like? Have they been gaining or losing share? As with consumer profiles, you might be able to add value to their responses by researching these facts up front.

Asking about a prospect's competition also has the added benefit that you can become an even better expert in the prospect's category. You might even hear about a new lead or two.

Examples of competition questions are:

- *"How do your sales compare with those of your competitors? Do you have any way of knowing or estimating whether your market share is growing or shrinking?"*
- *"Are there any newer businesses that are coming up fast?"*
- *"On a scale from one to ten, how would you rate your competitors' performance over the last six months?"*
- *"What do your competitors do better than you?"*
- *"Where are your competitors advertising? What media do they use and what strikes you as effective?"*
- *"If you stopped advertising right now, which one of your competitors would gain the most?"*

Current Partner Questions

Ideally, you were able to determine in advance of the first meeting what partner or partners (read: which of your competitors) the prospect is currently using. Ask in more detail about what's working and not working, what they are happy with or would like to change in their vendor relationships. How far in advance do they plan? What could change look like? Any new projects they are working on with their current partners?

Examples of partner questions are:

- *"What's the one major thing you would improve in your relationship with your current vendor?"*

- *"What are you trying to accomplish with your vendors in the next couple of months and this year?"*
- *"How satisfied are you with what you are getting? Where do you still have gaps?"*
- *"What's your media mix right now, and what's your strategy behind it?"*
- *"What initiatives have you already implemented to help with the issues you just mentioned?"*
- *"Have you ever had a promotional idea you really liked, but lacked the bandwidth to pull it off?"*
- *"What's the most successful strategic partnership with another company you had? What made it so special?"*

Sales Momentum Questions

The last category of questions is designed to help you gather valuable intelligence you need to advance the opportunity through the sales process. As with personal questions, you will find sales momentum questions even more effective if you are able to spread them out over the course of the meeting. These are questions in regard to timing (like budget planning or lead times), the decision-making process (including where the decision authority lies within the company), and results measurement.

Examples include:

- *"We covered a number of challenges. Let's prioritize them. What's the most urgent?"*
- *"How do you select your partners? What's the process, internally and externally? What are your decision criteria?"*
- *"Where are you in the process of evaluating options? What other alternatives are on the table?"*
- *"How are decisions being made internally for programs like these? Anyone else I should be speaking with? Who will be giving you input?"*
- *"How did you decide on a partner for this the last time around?"*
- *"Do you work with a creative, media, or PR agency? Do they need to get involved? When?"*

- *"How do you measure your marketing results? What systems do you have in place to measure advertising response? Is there anything you'd like to improve with your current attribution approach?"*
- *"When is your next campaign slated to start?"*
- *"Do you plan quarterly or monthly?"*

After you go through your questions, it is important to check with buyers if everything they think needed to be covered was in fact discussed:

"Is there anything else you think I should know? What else should we be talking about?"

CASE STUDY:
REBECCA GYMS DISCOVERY QUESTIONS

Here is a list of potential questions you prepared in advance of your video call with Rebecca Gyms CMO Tracy Ranner. This doesn't mean you will limit yourself to these questions or that you will in fact ask all of them. You definitely want to go deeper on some of the answers you will be receiving, especially the ones that uncover challenges Rebecca Gyms is facing right now. But the following questions are a good starting point:

- *"I read in* Crain's Business *that you have signed your lease for your first New York location in Williamsburg. How are your plans coming along for the other locations?"*
- *"My research shows that you have anywhere between ten to fifteen locations in each of the markets you are currently operating in. How many are you shooting for in New York?"*
- *"Will the majority of locations open at the same time, or will you have a staggered launch?"*
- *"There are several gym brands in the tristate area focused on female members only. Based on my research I believe Lucille*

Roberts is the largest one of them. How will you be different from them?"

- *"You have testimonials on your website from successful members of your West Coast locations. What would they say are the reasons they attend your gym? Why do they come to you?"*
- *"What's the biggest challenge you are facing from a marketing perspective for the launch?"*
- *"I noticed your current TV spots on the West Coast feature a Hispanic and an African American woman, both in their thirties or forties. Are there any consumer segments you will pursue more aggressively during your launch in New York?"*
- *"What does your ideal member look like? How old is she? What does she do for a living? How much money does she make? What type of person is she?"*
- *"Growing your female membership base quickly is, of course, crucial for a launch. But what are you mostly focused on to make that happen? Generating brand awareness? More social media followers? More tryouts?"*
- *"Based on Kantar data, the biggest marketing spenders with well-established brands in your category here are Planet Fitness, New York Sports Clubs, and Lucille Roberts. And, of course, apps like Variis or companies like Peloton are coming up strong. Who do you consider your top competitors? Where will your members come from?"*
- *"The majority of your ad dollars on the West Coast are spent on broadcast TV. Have you decided on your media mix for your New York launch?"*
- *"When you started at Rebecca Gyms last year, were you aware about this massive launch project on the East Coast? I am sure it must be long hours right now."*

- *"You mentioned that you are working with a PR agency. Are they based in New York? Are you working with a media agency as well?"*
- *"Have you locked in any influencers for your social media campaign yet?"*
- *"Who on your team is involved with marketing decisions for the launch? Anyone else I should be speaking with to gain even more insights?"*

TEACH

17

TEACH AND PERSONALIZE TO CONNECT WITH BUYERS

N ow that you have uncovered and prioritized the prospect's challenges and identified potential areas you and your company can be of help with, you are finally ready to share the information you put together in advance of the meeting.

This is the part of the first meeting that comes closest to what most people would understand under "selling." It is, however, smart selling, not the usual sales hyperbole around self-centered statements about the company, its products, and features. And it definitely is not a "capabilities presentation" showcasing everything your company is capable of, including sizzle reels or glossy brochures. Somehow, capabilities presentations have taken over the sales world, with marketing departments spending thousands of dollars on the most beautiful, animated presentations. They are sometimes so good that salespeople just skip the first three steps of a first meeting and jump right into the capabilities pitch, possibly even projecting it onto a big screen on a conference room wall. The problem is that this doesn't work in most first-meeting settings. If you are presenting to a larger group, like all the account teams of an advertising agency, be my guest—go for it. There is a time and a place for capabilities presentations. But the first meeting with a prospect is not it.

OFFER NEW PERSPECTIVES

Instead, sales champions bring insights, case studies, and research that has been customized for their prospects. They show what's working for the prospect's competitors. They offer details on new government regulations and market conditions. And they use the information they gathered during the discovery phase and focus on what they think will resonate the most and will be of greatest interest to the buyer.

This is also the part of the first meeting when you are trying to establish the fit between your company and theirs by connecting some of your company's assets and potential idea starters with the challenges prospects verbalized only a few minutes earlier. To do that, sales pros use stories, metaphors, and analogies instead of spec sheets, catalogs, and brochures. That could mean, for example, finding a connection between the mission statements of the two companies, the brand positioning of both, or their charity work.

Teaching prospects is all about offering them unique perspectives on their business, on how they can compete more effectively in their market, how they can drive revenue and free up operating expenses, or how they can reduce risk. As Matthew Dixon and Brent Adamson write in *The Challenger Sale*: "The Challenger rep moves customers out of their comfort zone by showing them their world in a different light." Their landmark study showed that the key characteristics defining a world-class sales experience are not related to how well salespeople can present their product or service, but to:

- Offering unique and valuable perspectives on the market
- Helping buyers navigate alternatives
- Providing ongoing advice or consultation

- Helping buyers avoid potential land mines
- Educating buyers on new issues and outcomes

Each of these attributes speaks directly to an urgent need of prospects not to *buy* something, but to *learn* something. What buyers are really saying is: *"Stop wasting my time trying to sell me. Challenge me. Teach me something new."*

PICK AND CHOOSE THE RIGHT MATERIAL

To bring the right information to the first meeting, you will have to make assumptions based on your research about prospects and their industry. You need to assume that prospects face similar challenges and have similar objectives as other companies in the same industry. You need to assume that marketplace dynamics are affecting them in a similar manner. Of course, not all of your assumptions will be accurate, but think about how much more effective this tactic is compared to you just rattling off stats about your product. Personalized information always wins.

If any of the material you brought to the meeting is irrelevant or might actually be detrimental to agreeing on a next step, just skip it and don't show it. That's exactly the reason why you start with your discovery questions *before* you go over your own material. Show the buyer that you actually listened.

In the Rebecca Gyms example, let's assume you had brought along information about a single, millennial on-air personality of one of your radio stations. She had agreed to act as a paid influencer during the Rebecca Gyms launch campaign, and you planned to run this idea by Tracy, the buyer. If, during the discovery phase of the meeting, you find out that Rebecca Gyms' member sweet spot is a mother in her late thirties or early forties, and as a result you don't feel that the suggested on-air personality is a good match for Rebecca Gyms, just skip over the information. Imagine, though, what would have happened if you had done it the other way around: presented the personality first and asked your discovery questions after. You would have wasted Tracy's time with something completely irrelevant, and would have lost credibility along the way.

This part of the meeting is also the right time to talk about what differentiates your company, product, or service. *"Here is what makes (name of company) different from other companies in the space."*

We already mentioned the analogy of painting a picture of the "neighborhood" before talking about the home. This is the time to do that. A good example of this approach in the radio business would be a slide with the headline *"Why Advertisers Are Seeing Success in the Audio Space Right Now."* Talk about the power of audio and the power of sound first, and then your radio brands.

LEAD WITH INSIGHTS

With permission from John Karpinski, executive vice president of Automotive Business Development and Partnerships at iHeartMedia, I am sharing two insights he put together for meetings with automotive prospects that accomplish everything I have suggested. John used both slides during a time when the country was slowly emerging from the COVID-19 related shutdowns.

Figure 17.1 provides prospects in the automotive category with a key piece of data, highlighting the fact that it takes car buyers an average of thirty-three days from the first website visit to actually making the purchase. This was extremely relevant information for dealers putting together marketing plans during this difficult time. In addition to teaching dealers, this information also creates a sense of urgency, which moves the sales process forward. *"So what you are saying is that if I want to sell cars in June, I should be advertising and driving shoppers to my website right now."*

Figure 17.2 features a study released by IBM during the COVID-19 crisis. It shows that the crisis significantly altered US consumer behavior regarding commuting to the office, with 48 percent of Americans saying they would use regular public transportation less or not at all. In other words, they would drive more, and as a result would need more cars. The salesperson's implicit message: *"Let's make sure they buy them from you. Oh, and by the way, more driving means more radio listening, so let's tell car shoppers about you on the radio."*

Why The Time to Advertise Is Now

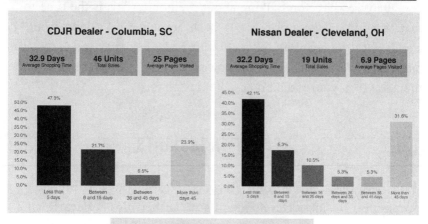

Figure 17.1: Leading with Insights in a First Meeting (1)

More Driving Means More Audio Consumption

IBM Study: COVID-19 Is Significantly Altering US Consumer Behavior
Personal Mobility Among the Areas Most Impacted

 48% Regular public transportation users say they will **USE Less or STOP USING**

 **50%** Would use these services **LESS or NOT AT ALL** post pandemic

 **25%** Say their personal vehicle will be their **EXCLUSIVE** transportation now

Figure 17.2: Leading with Insights in a First Meeting (2)

18

OVERVIEW OF FIRST-MEETING DECK

deally, the material you are showing the prospect is the exact opposite of the typical glossy brochure about your company or product. This might seem counterintuitive, but not for sales champions. Instead, follow these criteria for an engaging first-meeting deck:

- Open with a customized cover page that signals from the beginning this is a personalized presentation, not some generic deck or media kit. Leave your big company logo at the office; instead, include a picture that's relevant for prospects, either related to their category or themselves.
- Include insights and research that lead to, *"I never thought about it this way before"* and, *"Interesting, I didn't know that"* kinds of reactions with the prospect. The information presented needs to be sourced and, of course, relevant.
- Feature case studies from the same category or from companies facing similar market situations, including quotes from loyal customers.
- Connect your company with the buyer's company, thereby establishing a fit in the mind of the buyer.

- Sell the "neighborhood" before you sell the "home."
- Do not make it too long, certainly not longer than eight to ten pages, excluding the cover page.
- Do not include negative information about your competition and other vendors.
- Highlight how your company is different from the competition.
- Give a quick overview about the company and its process of working with customers.

DON'T SHOW YOUR SLIDES TOO EARLY

Leave your first-meeting deck in your briefcase until this phase of the first meeting. If you put it on the conference room table right at the beginning of the meeting, you run the risk of the buyer grabbing it, with the result of your suddenly having to go over the information you brought *before* the discovery phase of the meeting. That's not ideal.

When you shared your agenda at the beginning of the meeting, you let your prospect know that you would have information to share later in the meeting, so it shouldn't feel awkward that for the first three-quarters of the meeting you are not relying on any presentation material. Operating without a deck for the first part of the meeting helps you have real conversations with buyers. Once you walk them through your deck, try to make it as conversational as possible and ask more questions along the way.

PRINTOUTS OR BIG SCREEN?

Printouts are more effective in a first-meeting setting than projecting your slides onto a big screen. Usually when you use a screen, you will be tempted to set up your laptop before the meeting (which would make sense—you wouldn't want to do that in the middle of the meeting), with the cover page of your deck showing on the screen. However, much like putting your printout on the table right away at the beginning of the meeting, both you and your prospect will be distracted by it and turn to it too soon.

If your first meeting is conducted as a video call, don't put your deck up on the screen until this phase of the call, and take it down right after, to continue your conversation. Don't try to build rapport and conduct a client needs analysis with the buyer's face very small at the bottom of the screen, and the cover page of your deck—which you won't get to for thirty minutes—at the center of it.

CASE STUDY:
FIRST-MEETING DECK FOR REBECCA GYMS

Cover Page:
Mix of Rebecca Gyms branding and New York skyline. Small NYC Media logo. 80 percent Rebecca Gyms/20 percent NYC Media–focused design.

Page 2:
Consumer data about the New York fitness center market (such as average member profiles including age, ethnicity, borough, and household income; number of New York women not belonging to a gym in their core demo; etc.).

Page 3:
The competition: market shares, member profiles, positioning, number of locations, etc.

Page 4:
Advertising spend of key competitors including "home fitness" competitors like Peloton or Mirror; highlighting their most used media channels.

Page 5:
Case study of Y7 Studio launch from last year (Situation, Strategy, Results, Client Quote).

Page 6:

Building a connection between the missions of both companies. Potentially include both companies' work with UNICEF.

Slides 7 and 8:

Company overview: When presenting, focus on the assets you deem most important after all the information you received during the discovery phase.

Slide 9:

Partnering with NYC Media: The focus is on the process of campaign creation and execution as well as differentiators from other New York media companies.

Slide 10:

Idea Starters: Movement of New York women who hold each other accountable to work out on a consistent basis, led by female radio personalities and bloggers. Location-based digital targeting of Rebecca Gyms' main competitors like Lucille Roberts, with their members getting ads served while they are at the gym as well as after.

Slide 11:

Thank You and Next Steps

CLARIFY

19

WALKING AWAY WITH A CLEARLY DEFINED ASSIGNMENT

We are coming toward the end of the first meeting. This last phase is all about tying up loose ends and making sure you and the buyer are on the same page about everything that was discussed.

By now, you should have a pretty good idea if there is a "fit" between what your company can offer and what the prospect needs. Ask:

"From what we have shared with each other, I believe we can help with several of the challenges you mentioned. Do you agree?"

Listen closely, because the buyer's response will determine your next move. Pay attention to tone and excitement level in the person's voice. What does their body language tell you?

If you feel that buyers are not fully on board yet, you need to find a way to bring the reason or reasons for their hesitation out in the open:

"It seems you are having some concerns when it comes to talking about a next step. Tell me what's on your mind. I'd rather talk about it now than pretend they don't exist."

The last thing you want is to spend valuable time over the next few days or weeks working on a proposal for a prospect who did not fully buy into your process, your company, or you. Depending on the buyer's response, you need to decide your best approach to get back on track. You might have to walk the prospect through one more success story, ask a few more sales momentum questions, or test several other idea starters and see if they stick.

If buyers provide positive feedback, you are of course in an excellent position. Just don't get sloppy or lazy now. Don't start calculating your commission on the deal yet, as some of the more difficult work is still to come. We have all had great first meetings with buyers, only to come back to the office realizing that we are not 100 percent clear on the assignment we just received, or that we have no idea about the financial aspects of this potential deal.

Specifically, in the last phase of a first meeting, you need to:

- Decide which one of the challenges the buyer verbalized during the discovery phase your proposal and solution should address.
- Define in as much detail as possible what your solution should include and accomplish.
- Ask about and agree on a budget to be able to assemble a proposal that is tailored and realistic.
- Agree on and schedule a next step, most likely a follow-up meeting to present your proposal.

DECIDE ON FOCUS AREA

During the discovery phase, you help buyers verbalize their challenges and needs. If you took notes, you can now easily refer back to them and decide together on which project or projects you should start working. Don't be greedy now, though. You don't need to walk away with three different assignments after the first meeting. Narrow down the options and steer the buyer to the challenge you feel most confident you will be able to solve.

WHO DO WE WANT TO DO (OR TO BELIEVE) WHAT BY WHEN AND WHERE?

"Who do we want to do (or to believe) what by when and where?" is a concept marketing guru Scott Hopeck introduced me to a while ago. It is probably more relevant in the marketing and media world, and depending on the product or service you are selling, this approach might vary slightly. The point is to determine in detail what your solution needs to accomplish. If you did a good job with your discovery questions, you already have all of this information. All you need to do now is put it together in one concise statement and get the buy-in from the prospect.

The "who" refers to the target consumer. Think demographic, psychographic, or socio-economic information. The "what" is a desired behavior, like making a phone call, visiting a website, or downloading an app. The "believe" refers to a desired belief like an increase in brand loyalty or recognition. The "when" is all about the optimal time of the marketing campaign. And lastly, the "where" is about the location where the behavior takes place. It could be a store, online, or social channel.

In most cases, it will be beneficial for you to determine more than one measure of success. You will not always have full control of the results, and having more than one way to prove success in the execution phase gives you more flexibility when recapping results later on.

DETERMINE BUDGET

Sales champions have a cardinal rule they don't break: commit to work on proposals *only* if they are able to get clear direction from buyers about their budget for a specific assignment. It is way too risky to wait and save the conversation about price until the day you present your customized proposal. In fact, you don't want to talk about rates and costs too *soon* or too *late*. Too *early* in the first meeting runs the risk you won't have established enough credibility with the buyer and you will not receive an adequate assignment at all. Too *late* (in the proposal meeting) and your proposal might be completely off base money-wise.

Of all the steps of the sales process that you have to get right, this one is among the most difficult ones. It takes confidence and skill.

Tonality is again crucial. You need to come across matter of fact, as if you are having these types of conversations three times a day, instead of sounding overly excited or even nervous. Certainly don't say things like *"There is still one thing we need to talk about, and it's a big one—your budget for this assignment."* In short, don't make a big deal out of it.

Every sales situation is unique, and most differences you encounter from industry to industry probably occur in the last phase of the first meeting. It's hard to give specific examples in a more general B2B sales book like this one. I want to offer up two different approaches that I have seen work well, and then a third way in our Rebecca Gyms case study example.

Working Your Way Toward a Dollar Assignment

Figure 19.1 shows a fictional dialogue between a salesperson and a prospect, a step-by-step process that leads to a mutually agreed-upon budget for the assignment.

A good way to start the budget conversation with the buyer is with a sentence along the lines of:

"It's important for me to establish parameters for your campaign so I can build a program that delivers on what we just outlined. On a monthly (or quarterly or annual, depending on the type of prospect) *basis, how much do you want to invest to drive results?"*

It's possible that your prospect will completely ignore your question, so don't get thrown off by it. Talking about money is hard for many people. Many times, it will take further prompting and clarification. Work your way through the chart in Figure 19.1. You inquire about an investment range, and—if still unsuccessful—offer what in your experience is a high dollar amount for a comparable company in the prospect's industry. This is a very crucial point in your conversation. If the number you offer is too low, you

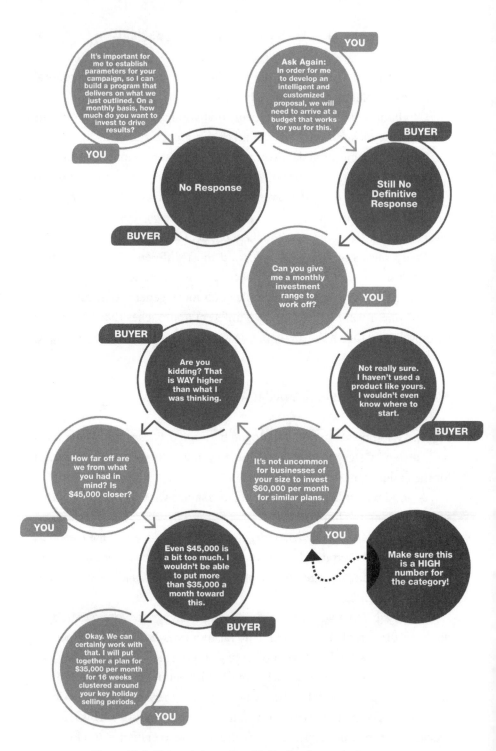

Figure 19.1: Determining a Specific Budget for an Assignment

potentially leave money on the table. If it is outrageously high, buyers will assume that you are not the category expert you led them to believe you are.

Make sure you always include the time period tied to an investment. You don't want to leave the meeting uncertain as to whether the agreed-upon investment level was monthly, quarterly, or even annual.

As you can see, it can sometimes be quite a battle to arrive at an investment amount with which both the buyer and you are comfortable.

An Investment, Not an Expense

You might have noticed how we used the terms "invest" and "investment" throughout the conversation shown in Figure 19.1. It is a positive word that people associate with some kind of return, and a much better option than words like "spend," "expense," or "cost."

Proactively offering investment *ranges* is usually *not* a good idea. *"We work with smaller clients who invest $2,000 a week, and larger customers with a budget of $30,000 a week"* will most likely result in your walking away with an assignment closer to $2,000 a week. Remember, you just met the prospect for the first time forty-five minutes ago. Despite your best efforts the prospect's radar is still set to "avoid risk first."

Sometimes, the investment verbalized by the buyer will be too low for you to come up with a solution that can achieve the desired outcome. You will need to be honest about it and address it right away. Leaving buyers with the impression that you will actually be able to work with the low amount discussed *and* deliver the results they have in mind is a recipe for disaster. Ask how a project like the one you are discussing is funded internally. Are there other departments that can chip in? Are there co-op dollars available the prospect can tap?

More Than One Option Is Usually a Bad Idea

Buyers might ask you to come back with *"a few options at different price points."* Try to not play that game. First, it causes more work on your end when you create your proposal. Second, it adds a level of complexity to it. Third, risk-averse buyers have a habit of leaning toward the lowest option salespeople are presenting, especially the first time around. Instead, explain to them that while all your solutions are fully customized, they are also scalable, and that you therefore will be presenting one solution that can then be scaled up or down. This also makes the process more efficient for buyers. If you state this with confidence, very rarely will you get an objection here.

Arriving at a Dollar Assignment Using Return on Investment Calculations

A different way to arrive at a budget is by following a more "bottom up"–driven approach that takes into account ROI considerations. This works especially well for higher-priced items, where it is easier to determine attribution and calculate how many new customers prospects need to gain for their investments to generate a certain amount of return. What you need to work out together with the buyer are:

* Lead Conversion Ratio: For example, how many phone calls turn into appointments and ultimately customers?
* Average Sale: What is the company charging customers on average?
* Gross Profit Margin: What's the profit percentage after labor (in service-oriented industries) or material (e.g., in retail)?
* Lifetime Value of a Customer: Do new customers come back for more, and how much is that worth on average?
* Expected Return of Investment: What is the prospect's investment in relation to the generated revenue (or savings)?

A simple math exercise can show buyers different investment options and will help you get buy-in to a number, or at least a range. This is a very effective method, especially when you know that the prospect has never used a product or service like yours before and you get the impression that they really want to help by giving you direction, but simply can't because of lack of expertise in this area.

Be Bold

I have also found success in unexpectedly asking for a prospect's budget during the discovery phase, woven in with all the other questions I was asking in the client needs analysis. In this scenario, I am typically not asking for the budget for my specific assignment because it would be too early for that, but I use a more general question such as, *"What's your total marketing budget for the Dallas market?"* If you say it confidently, as if it's a completely normal question in your line of work, you will be surprised how often you will get an actual response. Having that information is, of course, invaluable when determining the budget for the actual assignment later in the meeting.

SCHEDULE THE NEXT STEP

You have done everything right in your first meeting. Now you just have to determine and schedule the next step. This final stage of a first meeting is also the simplest. Just don't forget about it.

Of all fifty-six suitors Elaine Benes had in nine seasons of *Seinfeld*, one of the most annoying was Todd Gack. You might remember him as the guy who always claimed that he and Elaine "were *not* on a date." What Todd Gack did so well, though (with Elaine, and, later in the episode, with Jerry Seinfeld's model girlfriend), was to get agreement from the women on their next joint activity when they were still on their first date. He would ask about the second "date" in the middle of the first one, would even come up with bets that he knew he would lose, but that would guarantee him a follow-up dinner. And while I am of course not advocating that you cheat your way into the next meeting, my point is to always attempt to schedule it at the end of the first meeting.

Don't wait until you are back at the office, or—even worse—until you finish writing your proposal. In addition to committing the buyer to a specific date and time, it also puts you on the clock. Once the proposal meeting is scheduled, you can't procrastinate.

"What's the best next step?"

"What do you suggest is a good next step here?"

"Let's check our calendars and schedule a follow-up meeting."

Define responsibilities for follow-up work. Get the buyer involved by delegating certain tasks. The more you can do that, the more you get the buyer invested in the process. A mutual commitment is a good thing. You do this, I do that. Maybe the buyer is even willing to come in for a brainstorm meeting with your team. Whatever it is that will move the sales process forward, lock it in at this point.

One final thought as you are finishing the meeting and getting ready to leave: Act like a businessperson even in that moment. You have delivered a lot of value over the last forty-five minutes (or however long the meeting was). There's no need to thank the prospect three times for *"taking the time."* A confident, *"Great meeting you. Looking forward to working together more closely"* will do.

CASE STUDY:
CONFIRMING BUDGET AND NEXT STEP WITH
REBECCA GYMS

You: *"Tracy, this sounds like a great project to work on together and I feel good about us narrowing down all the different tactics and goals we discussed to a very clear lane and objective."*

Tracy: *"Yes, me too. Focusing on trial memberships is the way to go."*

You: *"You mentioned you got marketing dollars for the launch approved by your owner. Is all of it going toward generating trial memberships?"*

Tracy: *"The majority of it, yes, about 80 percent. The rest is mostly B2B-related stuff we have to do."*

You: *"Are you willing to look at a proposal from us for these 80 percent?"*

Tracy: *"I have already made a couple of commitments, but about two-thirds of it should be doable. Only if I like what you will be coming back with, of course. I am talking to several people."*

You: *"I am confident that you will. What are these two-thirds in dollars for the fourth quarter? I will need that to put together an intelligent plan."*

Tracy: *"About $800,000."*

You: *"Got it. I'll use that as a guideline when I go back to my team and brainstorm different campaign ideas. With an investment like that, how many trial memberships would you need to open?"*

Tracy: *"We know we won't be profitable in the first few months, but based on our plans I would expect you to deliver 1,500 trial memberships by the end of December."*

You: *"What's your conversion rate from online consultations—which you mentioned are your main way to sign up trial members—to actual trial memberships?"*

Tracy: *"In a new market, where our brand awareness is pretty much nonexistent, about one in four sign up, as long as our offer is competitive."*

You: *"Got it. That means we need to really drive traffic to your website and get about six thousand women to engage with your sales staff. That's about 0.2 percent of NYC Media's female audience. If we get the creative right, this should be doable. We also offer tools to measure brand awareness for launch campaigns. This will be an important metric for you as well. New Yorkers need to know about you first."*

Tracy: *"I agree. And yes, proving ROI will be extremely important. Rebecca Miller, our founder, is very focused on that. And so am I."*

You: *"Understood. It will take me about ten days to put everything together, especially since it involves several different spokespeople that will be part of this. In the meantime, can you please send me the information on the geographic locations you mentioned earlier? It will help with some of the geo-targeting tactics that will be part of the campaign."*

Tracy: *"I will do that. But please don't share these. They are still confidential."*

You: *"Of course. Let's check our calendars. Would the Thursday two weeks from today work for you?"*

Tracy: *"Yes, and I will actually be in New York that week. Maybe we can meet at your office? We don't have one yet. 2 PM work?"*

You: *"Sounds like a plan. Looking forward to it."*

20

CONFIRMING THE ASSIGNMENT

One easy way to stand out from the salespeople you are competing with is to follow up the first meeting with a thorough summary. It's important to send this email the same day to generate maximum impact. Don't wait until the next day, or a few days later. Send it the same day.

My guess is about half the salespeople don't send a follow-up note to a buyer at all, and of the ones that do send one, 75 percent send a one-liner, telling the buyer how great it was to meet him and (here we go again) to thank him for his time. That's it.

ELEMENTS OF EFFECTIVE FOLLOW-UP EMAILS

Follow-up emails of sales champions, on the other hand, include the following:

- A summary of the challenges you uncovered.
- The one or two challenges your proposal will try to solve.

- "Who do we want to do (or to believe) what by when and where?" or something similar that spells out the objective of your solution.
- Any assets or idea starters buyers explicitly mentioned as something that they would like to see included in the proposal.
- The budget for your customized solution that the buyer and you determined together.
- Permission to call them in advance of the meeting to clarify information and potentially run some initial ideas by them. This is a very good tactic to keep the buyer engaged in the process. It will also help you avoid unwanted surprises during the upcoming presentation of your proposal.
- A link to the first meeting deck you presented. Ideally, you use tools like ClearSlide that not only help you avoid clogging up the buyer's email in-box, but also allow you to track if your deck was opened or shared with other people. If for some reason you don't have access to such tools, attach a PDF file to your email, not a PowerPoint file. Make sure your links and files are named properly. *"ProspectVersion23b_notypos"* will not do.
- State the date, time, and location for the next meeting, and that you will send out a meeting invitation in a separate email.

Pretty involved, right? Yes, but absolutely worth it! If you do this right, replies like *"Thank you for being so thorough"* or *"Excellent, this captures all the important points we discussed. Absolutely feel free to call me if you have questions in the meantime"* will become the norm and not the exception.

It's also absolutely possible that you might have misunderstood something during the meeting. Your email allows buyers to correct you. Sometimes these corrections will involve the budget amount, and that's absolutely okay. Maybe buyers didn't feel comfortable correcting you in person; maybe they spoke to other decision makers or influencers in the company after your meeting and changed their mind. Whatever the reason, it's good to get these misunderstandings out in the open now, and not in the middle of your upcoming proposal presentation.

CASE STUDY:
CONFIRMATION EMAIL TO REBECCA GYMS

Subject: Recap of our call / Next steps

Tracy,

It was great connecting with you this morning. With a high of 33 degrees here in New York, I would have loved to do the meeting in person in San Diego instead of on Microsoft Teams.

Here are some of my key takeaways:

- *Rebecca Gyms launch planned in New York for Q4, most likely in November.*
- *Six locations should be open at that point.*
- *Core member is a mid- to high-income female, 35–50 years old, most likely a mom living in the five boroughs or suburbs who wants to work out or attend class right after work, before going home.*
- *Positioned more upscale than main competitor Lucille Roberts. Rebecca Gyms will offer more modern facilities and more yoga, cycling, dance, and boxing classes with unlimited access.*
- *Monthly membership fee will be about 50 percent higher than Lucille Roberts.*
- *The new app is launching in September.*
- *Key challenges:*
    - *Brand completely unknown on the East Coast*
    - *Fitness category in New York already crowded, including new home fitness offerings*
    - *Rebecca Gyms app has not launched yet and will initially have less content than some of the competitors*
    - *Need to get off to good start, with generating interest in trial memberships identified as the core challenge*

Campaign Objective: *In what ways can we motivate thirty-five- to fifty-year-old, high-income moms to open trial memberships online for the six Rebecca Gyms locations in November / December, thereby exceeding Rebecca Gyms' goal of 1,500 trial memberships by December 31.*

- *Interested in pursuing influencer program on-air / magazine / social, but needs to be personality who resonates with target member base.*
- *Campaign success measured on trial memberships, web traffic, brand awareness.*
- *Campaign budget: $800,000*

Please let me know if I understood everything correctly. And <u>click here</u> to access the slides we went over today.

<u>*Next steps:*</u>

- *We will connect with potential influencers based on the feedback you gave us, and from there build out a media plan that generates reach quickly and cost-efficiently.*
- *Tracy to send over the information on the geographic Rebecca Gyms locations planned for the launch.*
- *I will give you a call after our internal brainstorm meeting with our creative team and our producers, to check if we are on the right track.*

I am looking forward to meeting you in person on Thursday, May 22, at 2 PM EST at our offices. A conference room is already reserved and we will make sure to introduce you to some of our talent and potential influencers for your campaign. I will send you an Outlook invite with address information separately.

Looking forward to working together on this.

Dave Gahan

PRESENT

21

CREATING PROPOSALS THAT CONVINCE

reat job! You have established the buyer's perception that your company, product, or service fits the criteria the buyer has for a future partner. You have also positioned yourself as someone with whom the buyer wants to work. Your proposal needs to reinforce and confirm these perceptions. Because it is often the first tangible evidence buyers have of your ability to solve their problems, it must make good on the promises made during your previous contacts and interactions.

If your proposals are prospect-centric, creative, and insightful, buyers will assume that's what working with you will be like. If they are not, they may assume that the "real" you is what they see in the proposal, not what they heard from you in the first meeting.

FRONTLOAD YOUR EFFORT

When should you start working on the proposal? Many salespeople set the information they received in the first meeting aside and work on other projects and clients. Then, a couple of days before the date of the presentation, they frantically begin and work late into the night before the meeting. That's a big mistake!

The best time to work on a proposal is right after you confirmed and clarified the assignment with the buyer. Not only is everything you discussed still fresh in your mind, it will also give other people on your team who help with ideation, creation, or research more time to plan. And it will make it easier to involve the buyer in the process. This type of "front-loading" allows you to control the effort rather than letting the effort control you. Doesn't it feel great to have a fully built proposal printed out on your desk a week before the proposal meeting?

DON'T UNDERESTIMATE THE IMPORTANCE OF A HIGH-QUALITY PROPOSAL

Proposals don't usually win a deal, but they can lose them in a heartbeat. The document you end up presenting might actually do more harm than good. It might not be fair, but we judge someone's ability to deliver products or services by the quality of the proposal they submit. The problem is that many salespeople don't know what a great proposal looks like. They think it is about giving the prospect a ton of information. They lose sight of the audience and start writing to themselves. Or they forget that the jargon and acronyms they are using with their colleagues around the office are incomprehensible to a buyer.

A proposal is not an isolated creation, but a critical part of a larger process. It helps you sell, but it shouldn't sell for you. *You* have to do that. Your written proposal is just the outline. You provide the details in conversation. This is important and we will revisit this concept in chapter twenty-two, when we will go over how to most effectively *present* a proposal to a buyer. Proposals are props to help you make the best business case you can for the buyers to work with you.

PROPOSALS NEED TO FIT THE SALES SITUATION

Proposals come in many shapes and forms, depending on which industry you are in. It obviously makes a huge difference if you are selling a $10,000 advertising schedule to a family-owned small business or if you are working for a sophisticated aerospace and defense contractor bidding on a government contract, using special internal proposal centers staffed with proposal managers, writers, graphic designers, and other specialists. These latter assignments will be part of a more comprehensive Request for Proposal process, which goes way beyond the scope of this book. We will stay focused on new business sales situations where you connected with a prospect you found and researched, received a specific assignment, and will now create and present the solution to the challenges you uncovered.

WHAT MAKES PROPOSALS EFFECTIVE

Great proposals are prospect oriented—they are oriented toward *them*, meet *their* needs, address *their* problems, use *their* terminology, and present the offer in terms of how it benefits *them*.

Effective proposals persuade in many ways:

- They work on the intuitive and subliminal level as much as they do on the rational, descriptive level. They don't just sell the sizzle, they sell the sizzle and the steak. They build an emotional connection, then confirm it with data. They make the right brain and the left brain work together. A great proposal says, in effect, *"I understand your challenge and know what you need. I have a creative but simple solution that will work for you and solve the issue. And I have the data to back up my claims."* In a best-case scenario, prospects will feel like they are reading their own thoughts.
- First and foremost, proposals are sales documents. They must sell, not just tell. They have to sell your solution, your expertise,

your process. Chris Lytle, in his book *The Accidental Salesperson*, compares an effective proposal with a good TV infomercial that first sets forth the problem, then explains the solution, and finally demonstrates how the product best provides the solution. It also offers proof of the claim by making clear that the buyer is not alone, with thousands (or even millions) of people having turned their lives around with the advertised product.

- They don't just list specifications and features your company brings to the table. Instead, they tell a compelling story, one that helps buyers see your solution in a more insightful and interesting way than they had previously imagined. It is a story that builds trust and confidence. It is a story that engages buyers first by focusing on them, their problems and needs, and then weaves in the salesperson's solution. It shows how it addresses the problem in a convincing way and elegantly states how the solution is better than competing solutions, including the current one the buyer uses. A great story told poorly will lose to a good story told well every time.

- With larger opportunities, you are likely to find that an entire team makes the buying decision, and that you may never have the opportunity to meet with and present your proposal to every member of the team. As David Pugh and Terry Bacon write in their book *Powerful Proposals*, a great proposal gives buyers what they need to sell your solution when they go down the hall to make their recommendation to their boss, the final decision maker, or potentially even the board of directors. The minute they do that, they become virtual members of your business development team and need to be armed with the most compelling document possible—one they can present internally as is, without reformatting or rewriting.

- Their creative page designs draw the reader in and make comprehending the solution and offer much easier. A decade ago, this might have been less important, and buyers were willing to overlook poor design if the solution itself was good. That's no longer true. Sophisticated prospects expect professional design, and they will deduct many points if your proposal lacks one.

- They are concise and uncomplicated. Unnecessary complexity is always detrimental to moving the sale forward. You are dealing with overwhelmed, stressed-out buyers, who—if things get too complicated—will zone out. And that's the last thing you want to happen during a proposal presentation. An effective proposal should only include as much content as the decision maker needs. Ease of evaluation is a very real factor of success.
- They keep the amount of boilerplate used in the proposal to a minimum. Boilerplate is standardized text or graphics, recycled material that was used in previous proposals and copied over. Sometimes it does make sense to include it in a proposal to save time, but we all know of a colleague who forgot to change the previous prospect's name when the new proposal was presented. Awkward! Sophisticated buyers can pick up on boilerplate. As a rule, the less boilerplate is used, the higher the quality of the proposal.
- They speak with one voice, even if several people worked on them. I am always stunned by how often salespeople copy and paste one-sheets from different sources into their proposals, with no regard to formatting them to look like one cohesive document. Make the effort to ensure its style and tone have a single voice.

THE BEST PROPOSALS ARE CUSTOMER FOCUSED

Take a moment and review the last five proposals you created. Use a red marker to flag all content that relates to your own company (like price lists; company history; market shares in your industry; one-sheets about products/assets; company-related pictures like staff, building, or logo) and a green marker to note all content that relates to the prospect (like challenges, goals, solution strategies, and potential outcomes). Quite eye-opening, right? If you are like most salespeople, red will dominate green by at least 3:1. Too many salespeople think that their company and product literature are important sales tools. They are not. Buyers don't care, particularly the ones who lack in-depth knowledge of what you are offering. They just want to understand what you can do for them.

Poorly written proposals are "we" focused instead of "you" focused. They are self-involved and focus on capabilities. The best proposals, on the other hand, link everything to the prospect's goals, needs, and requirements. In a customer-focused proposal, the seller's capabilities are the means to the customer's end. They highlight how great you can make the prospect's business, not how great your business is. Buyers buy benefits, not features. A good way to cross-check your proposals is to run them through the "so what?" filter. Your prospects certainly will when you walk them through the proposal.

OWN THE PROPOSAL GENERATION PROCESS

From the audience to the content to the formatting, each part of a winning business proposal requires thoughtful planning and development. Sometimes you will do all that yourself; other times you will collaborate with other departments and colleagues, where you will function more like the conductor of an orchestra, making sure everyone is working together well, knows their responsibilities and tasks, and delivers their parts of the proposal on time. Don't lose control of the process here. You have to be the one who owns it and takes ultimate responsibility. It is you, after all, who owns the deal, who will be presenting the final document to the buyer, and who ultimately gets paid.

QUALITY CONTROL

Using the outcomes of brainstorms with people on your and other teams, you might build your solution from scratch. Or you might use one of the idea starters you already discussed with the buyer in the first meeting and just build it out as a full-blown concept. And sometimes, buyers are really enamored with an idea they themselves had floated during the first meeting and want to see more details on it. Wherever the ideas came from, once your proposal is finished, make sure you have a colleague or your manager look it over. They will bring a fresh eye to the document and its ability to persuade. This "removed examination" ensures that the proposed solution and supporting materials are understandable and visually appealing. Salespeople who write the proposal can sometimes be too close to it, and this extra step acts as a necessary quality control mechanism.

Not too long ago, a salesperson invited me along to a seven-figure new business pitch to a digital start-up that had just gotten an enormous amount of funding. The proposal was well structured and visually appealing, and the presentation and discussion went well. I was really impressed by how the salesperson handled himself. When we got to the last couple of pages of the proposal, though, everything went downhill fast. The salesperson, or whoever created the proposal, had clearly copied some of the data on deliverables from an outdated file, and as a result none of the numbers presented added up. Numbers for impressions, reach, and frequency were off, dates were wrong, and some of the pricing was inaccurate. All the hard work that went into the proposal and all the time that was invested into the prospect relationship was jeopardized by one rookie mistake all the way at the end of the sales process. While the deal did eventually close (although at a lower level), this mistake was a major setback and ended up costing the salesperson a significant amount of commission.

The lesson here is that as visually appealing as your proposal can look, your proposed solution must also be accurate. Triple-check timelines, budget values, material amounts, hourly estimates, rates, and other specifics. This verification ensures that what you are offering the client in the proposed solution is correct. An incorrect statement could cost your company—and you—a lot of money.

"Bad spellers of the world—untie," one of my sales managers used to say. And to this day, typos in well-thought-out proposals drive me crazy. You have worked so hard to come this far with a prospect; don't drop the ball now by not being detail oriented. A proposal must be free of grammatical and spelling mistakes. They are inexcusable. If you are not sure of a word or phrase, check with the spelling and grammar tools in Microsoft Word or on grammarly.com.

PROPOSAL TEMPLATES CAN SAVE TIME

When creating a new proposal, writing it is actually the last thing you should do. First, determine the content, solution, structure, and layout. Then start writing.

Starting to work on a proposal can feel a little overwhelming. Yes, you are excited about the opportunity to do business with a potential new customer. But writing an effective proposal takes focus and time. Newer salespeople will need a lot of help from their sales managers, and that's okay. It's one of the core responsibilities of sales managers to arm their sales force with proposal layouts and proposal templates customizable for each unique sales situation. There is no need to reinvent the wheel each time you create a proposal, and a well-organized template can save valuable time for similar projects. A word of caution here, though: in the wrong hands, templates can easily morph into generic proposals, so make sure your proposal process is both efficient and effective.

WRITING WITH THE AUDIENCE IN MIND

To ensure your proposal is as powerful as possible, prepare, plan, write, and review with the proposal audience in mind. The audience is the most crucial factor to get right when creating the proposal. The writer must understand the reader on the other side of the document. What is their role? Are they the decision maker? Will they share the proposal with others? If yes, who? What are the buyers' main concerns? What is their background? The audience, not the author, drives the design.

WHAT NEEDS TO BE INCLUDED IN A PERSUASIVE PROPOSAL

Effective proposals differ significantly across industries and sales situations, but here are some components that most proposals should include:

- A client-centric cover page with a title that says more than just "Proposal for XYZ Company." Think again about the audience and what type of headline would grab their attention. It should be snappy and engaging, and can be a one-line overview of the entire proposal or the challenge itself (*"How to . . ."*). If you're unsure of the title, don't worry; you can compose it after writing the proposal. That may even be a better time to title the document, as the writing process may inspire the perfect title.

- A quick and easy-to-read list of bullet points that captures the key facts relevant to the solution as well as challenges you uncovered in the first meeting. Examples of potential headlines for this slide are *"Our Knowledge of Your Situation," "Our Understanding of Your Status Quo,"* or *"What You Told Us."* If you did a thorough job in your follow-up email of the first meeting, you should be able to just copy most of the information over from there. The very fact that you can list these issues shows that you understand the prospect's business. Definitely also include the project's budget or at least the budget range that you and the buyer discussed in the first meeting. This is a game changer! Think about how much pressure and friction this move takes out of the meeting. No need for the buyer to jump to the last section of the proposal to find out the total cost of the solution you are proposing; no skepticism throughout the meeting that your concept might not be affordable. This slide is important for another reason: it gives the prospect the opportunity to correct some of the facts listed. Maybe you misunderstood, maybe things changed since your first meeting and your confirmation email. But it is better to find out about these changes at this stage of your presentation rather than at the end.

- The objective of the project or solution summarized in detail; for example, by using the "Who do we want to do (or to believe) what by when and where?" approach outlined in chapter nineteen.

- The Concept/The Idea/The Strategy: However you title this slide, it is probably the most important slide of the entire proposal, where you—in an easy-to-understand and concise way—introduce your recommended solution and give an overview of the project.

We will cover in the next chapter how we will present this slide to buyers, but know for now that it is the slide where the real selling will happen. This is when you look your buyers straight in the eye and explain what you and your team came up with and why your idea will work. As a result, this slide should be visually very appealing but not too wordy.

- A "Plan of Execution" slide that includes details about how the concept will be brought to life. It covers timeline, staffing, assets used, and so on. Ideally, this is presented in a very comprehensive way that proves you have thought through everything and are an expert in executing these types of projects.

- Measurement of Project Success: Buyers want to know how they can track progress and ROI on what you are proposing. It's important you think this through, as this question is guaranteed to come up at one point of the proposal meeting. Don't avoid it. Be proactive, embrace it, and address it with the buyer on your terms.

- Your Power Story: A quick summary of why your partners work with you, as covered in chapter fourteen. Especially in a competitive situation that pits you against other companies, it will also be necessary to highlight key differentiators against your competition. Clearly, this section is about your company and not the prospect, so make sure it is still worded in a customer-centric way. Including your power story shortly before the end of the proposal ensures buyers remember what type of caliber of a company they are about to partner with.

- Any research or insights that support the expected success of your solution. Buyers are looking for logical justifications to minimize risk and justify emotionally-based decisions they made when you walked them through your creative concept.

- Summary of Deliverables and Investment: Shows everything you will be delivering in detail and states the total investment for the proposed solution. It should also give an expiration date for the quoted rates to create urgency on the side of the buyer. In many industries, the proposal doubles as a contract, in which case this page should include terms and conditions and space for a signature. If warranted, include a copyright notice, usually consisting of the word "copyright" or the symbol, date, author's name, and statement of rights.

MAKE READING YOUR PROPOSAL EASY

As readers, we all know what we like: conciseness, clarity, simplicity. Unfortunately, too often when we sit down to write, we fail to create anything like that. We produce lengthy, verbose, and complicated documents. Here are a few tips for improving proposal readability:

- Use the active voice. It is stronger and easier to read and should be the natural choice for business proposal writing. An example of a passive sentence is "The materials will be delivered to the site by our operators." Worded as an active sentence, it would be "Our operators will deliver the materials to the site."
- Mark Twain said that adjectives are bad and verbs are good: "Every time you use the word 'very,' use 'damn' instead. Your editor will take out the 'damn.'"
- Simple wording will ensure the text stays accessible. The general rule is to keep the sentence structure simple. The more clauses and phrases you add to a sentence, the greater your risk of being misunderstood. As always, keep the audience in mind and write in the simplest terms appropriate for the reader.
- A common mistake in proposals is writing to sound impressive. Yes, proposals need to impress the reader, but for the right reasons. Extravagant or highly technical text actually causes the reader to be less engaged. It is more difficult to understand and therefore less effective at communicating the information.
- White space is pleasing to the eye. It appears sleek and modern, and makes the text accessible. Large blocks of text or content without white space makes a document feel cluttered. The reader gets overwhelmed with information and can start to skim.

- Lists, bullet points, and tables add value to your proposal. A list presented within a sentence will be less readable than one shown as a bulleted list.
- Graphics can improve readers' understanding. They can also be so poorly designed or flashy that they detract from the proposal. What you absolutely want to avoid are cheesy stock images, disproportionately scaled images, and pixelated low-resolution images. Used correctly, though, graphics can help make a positive impression.

CASE STUDY:
PROPOSAL OUTLINE FOR REBECCA GYMS

Over the past couple of weeks, you connected twice with Tracy Ranner about suggestions for potential spokespeople for Rebecca Gyms. Some of them are on-air talent of your female-targeted radio stations, others are contributors for NYC Media's digital properties with large social media followings. Because of her involvement in the selection process, Tracy won't be surprised by the strategic direction of your proposed campaign.

Cover Page:
Title: *"NYC's Newest Women's Fitness Movement"*
Sub-headline: *"A Campaign Built to Exceed Rebecca Gyms' Trial Membership Goals for Its New York Launch"*

Page 2:
"Our Understanding of Rebecca Gyms' Launch Strategy": Summarizes the main information you gathered during the first meeting and on your most recent phone calls. It includes Rebecca Gyms' positioning in the marketplace, its competitive situation, and its key

challenges during the launch phase in New York. It also clearly states the budget assignment you received from Tracy in the first meeting: $800,000 for a November/December campaign.

Page 3:

"Campaign Objective": To motivate thirty-five to fifty-year-old high-income moms to open trial memberships online for the six New York Rebecca Gyms locations in November/December, exceeding Rebecca Gyms' goal of 1,500 trial memberships by December 31.

Page 4:

"The Concept: Introducing NYC's Newest Women's Fitness Movement": High-level overview of the campaign, including introduction of the three female influencers you selected and how NYC Media will bring this "controlled PR" campaign to life on air and on its digital and social properties. The slide is fully focused on content integration, and not on advertising impressions. You are selling the sizzle here and trying to connect Tracy emotionally with the campaign.

Page 5:

"Meet the Rebecca Gyms Spokespeople": Expand on why you chose the three influencers for this campaign. Make this client-centric, more than just a "bio."

Page 6:

"Generate Reach Quickly by Using the Power of Audio": The proposal is transitioning to the more detail-oriented execution of the plan and will cover the radio stations on which and the times during which the on-air announcements will be heard.

Page 7:

"Amplify the Message Digitally": Describes how the campaign will use NYC Media's digital and social platforms to bring the

program to life and includes the different digital ad formats that will be used.

Page 8:

"Trial Membership Conquest from the Competition": The slide explains how the campaign will use location-based digital targeting and data to reach thirty-five- to fifty-year-old moms on location at their current fitness centers like Lucille Roberts and after they leave.

Page 9:

"Campaign Timeline": Graphically shows all campaign elements and their duration as part of a timeline that is divided into eight weeks, highlighting key milestones of the campaign.

Page 10:

"Delivering Results and ROI": A consumer-purchase funnel graphic, starting at the top with "brand awareness" and ending at the bottom with "action" (in our case the opening of a trial membership), shows at which stage of the funnel each of the tactics used will be effective. The slide also states how we will measure website traffic attributed to the on-air campaign as well as conversion rates of the location-based digital conquest campaign.

Page 10:

"What Makes Us Different from Other Media Companies": You know that Tracy is also speaking with other potential launch partners, and as a result you will, in a very elegant and not boastful way, highlight what makes NYC Media unique. A lot of this information will come from your power story, and ideally it follows its example of stating benefits in a very client-centric way.

Page 11:

"Campaign Deliverables and Investment": This slide details every-thing Rebecca Gyms will receive from NYC Media over the course of the campaign. It lists every daypart, every asset, all impressions, and other items. The more, the better. You want to show that Rebecca Gyms receives a ton for the net investment that is also stated on this slide: $794,500.

Page 12:

"Thank You and Next Steps": Since at this investment level you will have to get your legal department involved, you are mentioning it as a next step, together with the discussion of campaign creative.

22

PROPOSAL MEETINGS AS SALES DIALOGUES

There is nothing better than walking into a meeting with a buyer knowing you have a killer proposal in hand that includes a killer idea. You can't wait to share your concepts and ideas and move the sale forward, potentially even closing the deal in the same meeting. On the flipside, we have all had to deal with the uneasy pit in our stomach caused by the boring, below-average proposal we were about to present.

"Pitching" is one of those tasks in the sales process most people connect with "being in sales." We picture an energetic person standing at the head of the table in a boardroom setting, running through PowerPoint slides in presentation mode, delivering a monologue that mentions all the key information about the salesperson's company and product. Sales champions, of course, know better than to do that.

Sales presentations are meant to be two-way conversations, dialogues between you and the buyer. Yes, salespeople will talk more than in the first meeting and will take the lead in the conversation, but the more they can turn the presentation into a dialogue—by checking in after every section and by asking questions—the more effective the meeting will be. A conversation beats a presentation every time.

The sales world uses different terminologies for this type of meeting: "presentation meeting," "ask meeting," "pitch meeting," "proposal meeting," and several others. To me, the words "presentation" and "pitch" always sounded too much like a one-way conversation. And "ask meeting" is a little bit misleading, because—as you will find out in chapter twenty-three—an effective salesperson really should be "asking" throughout the entire sales process. You should ask for a meeting, for information, for an assignment, for the order. Instead, we will use the term "proposal meeting" in this book.

A proposal meeting is actually one of the easier steps in the sales process. It is certainly easier than the first meeting. The awkwardness of meeting someone for the first time is gone. Hopefully you have established a connection with the buyer and found commonalities. Even the surroundings at their location will look familiar. Ideally, you also involved the buyer in some way while creating the proposal. Because of the nature of a proposal meeting, it's usually also easier to control. And, as with anything else, the more proposal meetings you have, the more presentations you give, the better you will get.

When Things Go Wrong

Ask anyone about the worst proposal presentations they have been part of, and they will probably tell you:

- The presenter just read from the slides.
- The presenter didn't interact with the audience.
- The presenter droned on even though no one was listening.

All of these issues have the same cause. One of the fundamental blunders salespeople make during proposal meetings is that they focus too much on themselves. If you follow the guidance in this book, your written proposal is already built in a very prospect-centric way, which almost forces you to focus more on the prospect than yourself. But make sure this self-centeredness doesn't creep in during the proposal meeting. Phrases like *"We are great at,"* *"You will be dealing with the best,"* and *"There is no one better than"* have no place in a seed email, no place in the first meeting, and no place in the proposal meeting.

Another mistake salespeople frequently make is simply wanting the deal to happen too much. They want to close it right now, in this second, and they become impatient. This in itself is not the problem. It's when this desperation becomes obvious to buyers that proposal meetings start to go downhill.

Paul Boross, the "Pitch Doctor," in his book *The Pitching Bible*, defines the objective of a proposal meeting as follows:

"To get the message across as clearly and as strongly as I can, and to make sure that before I leave the room, the audience absolutely understands my proposal and how it is different to my competitors' proposals."

As you can see, his goal doesn't explicitly state things like "closing the deal" or "getting to yes."

Yes, you want the order. But don't put too much pressure on yourself. Focus on the basic blocking and tackling of an effective proposal meeting, and if you execute all tactics well, good things will happen. If that means an additional, unexpected step that gets you closer to making the sale, but doesn't yet result in the order itself, so be it. I understand that it can be very difficult to give up the need to control the result. But, in doing so, you might come to realize that you have gained more control over the result itself.

THREE ELEMENTS OF A SUCCESSFUL PROPOSAL MEETING

For a proposal meeting to go well, there are three elements you have to master:

- WHERE: the environment
- WHAT: the content
- HOW: your presentation style

MASTER THE WHERE

Many external factors can make a proposal meeting a success or drag it down, from the room you are meeting in and its temperature and lighting, all the way to the participants themselves and their seating arrangements. Some things you can control, others not.

All the World Is a Stage, and Most of Us Are Desperately Unrehearsed

What is absolutely in your control is to arrive to the proposal meeting fully rehearsed. It doesn't matter if you have twenty-five years' or two months' sales experience: practicing your sales presentation not just once, but several times, is mandatory. Ideally, do it with an audience, not just by yourself at your desk. Ask your manager or one of your colleagues to stand in as the buyer, and have them give you feedback on your delivery. The buyer should not be the first person to hear your presentation. You also need to have a very good idea about how long your presentation is, and to remember the order of your slides. A dress rehearsal will accomplish both.

Proposal Meeting Conditions

In addition to role-playing in preparation for the proposal meeting, you must be completely clear on several other questions:

- Where is the meeting taking place? If it will be held at the prospect's location, which room will you be in: a conference room (preferably, since it's a more neutral space and allows you to arrive early), in the buyer's office (not ideal at all, since you have to present your proposal across the desk), or in the cafeteria (problematic if your proposal includes sound and video elements)?

Hosting the prospect at your own office, of course, is what you want to shoot for; the environment is much easier to control. We already covered the intricacies of a Zoom or Microsoft Teams meeting in chapter thirteen.

- Will you be projecting onto a screen or will you hand out hard copies? While I personally prefer printouts for most first meetings with buyers, my preference for proposal meetings is to project onto a screen. It increases your control over the meeting and prevents buyers from skipping ahead, which can derail even the best-rehearsed meetings. As mentioned in chapter thirteen, sit closest to the screen if you use a projector.

- Who will be attending the meeting? Many times, buyers will invite additional team members to the proposal meeting. What's their background? What's their role? Try to find out as much as you can in advance. Then, decide how you can get the new participants up to speed quickly about your assignment, your company, and you. Sometimes that might mean a separate meeting before the proposal meeting. Other times, it might mean giving a more detailed summary of the assignment and potentially going over your power story at the beginning of the proposal meeting.

Arrive Early

If your meeting is in a conference room at the prospect's location, try to arrive at least twenty minutes early. That leaves you enough time to check the physical surroundings of the room. It allows you to rearrange some of the seating, and—if needed—close the blinds, change the thermostat, and adjust the lighting. Arriving early also allows you to check if all the equipment works properly. If not, you have enough time to ask for IT help. Ideally, your customized cover page is already projected onto the big conference room screen when your buyer arrives.

Define Your Team Members' Roles

If you are presenting your proposal together with several people on your team—a very common practice in the advertising agency and media world—make sure each team member's role is clearly defined in advance, and that everyone knows when during the presentation they must speak and for how long. This last point is important. We have all been part of presentations that went way too long because every single speaker was just a little bit over. These extra minutes add up quickly.

Embrace Public Speaking by Working the Room

The five minutes leading up to the proposal meeting can be some of the most productive sales minutes of the entire meeting, especially if you are presenting to team members on the prospect's side you had not met yet. Network. Build rapport. Work the room. Introduce yourself. Make small talk. This is not the time to make last-minute changes to your proposal or to answer emails. Your hosts have to be your full priority. You want to speak with every person in the room *before* you start the meeting.

This has a side benefit. Even confident salespeople can get a little tense and nervous before a presentation. It's the usual fear of public speaking. Most of us have it. Remember the old Jerry Seinfeld joke: "According to most studies, people's number one fear is public speaking. Number two is death. This means to the average person, if you go to a funeral, you're better off in the casket than doing the eulogy." Build rapport in the minutes before the meeting to make your speaking less "public," and turn your presentation into more of a conversation with people you already know. It will make you feel more confident and comfortable.

MASTER THE WHAT

In communicating your content, you want to transfer emotion as well as impart information. You need to bring your written proposal to life. And the best way to do this is to look at the written proposal as nothing more than props, similar to how stage actors and actresses use props to deliver their lines more effectively. They address the audience directly, and use props as needed for support. Unfortunately, most salespeople do the exact opposite and stick way too closely to the written proposal, literally reading entire sections.

Before you start your presentation, officially introduce your team. If new people from the prospect side joined, make sure to ask them to introduce themselves, including their role and responsibilities within the company. That will help you tailor your presentation and focus on some people more than others during certain sections.

Most presentations should follow the classic structure: tell them what you are going to tell them, tell them, and then tell them what you told them.

Open Strong

The opening is important. You should briefly explain:

- What the audience can expect.
- What's in it for the buyers.
- What you are going to talk about.
- How long you estimate the presentation will be.
- When the audience can ask questions (to make the presentation as conversational as possible, you should invite them to *"ask anytime"*).
- What they will walk away with by the end of the presentation.

Then, you summarize the main details from the first meeting and confirm that all assumptions and information, as well as the detailed objective of the campaign, are still on point and relevant. You know from the previous chapter that right at the beginning, your proposal includes the dollar assignment you agreed upon with the prospect in the first meeting. Don't be shy now and skip over this. It's important to know if this budget amount is still accurate. If it is not, you will have to make a decision. If your solution is easily scalable, mention that to the buyer and continue the presentation, then deal with the budget issue at the end of the meeting. If you know that your proposed solution would simply not be doable at a lower price point, you will have to improvise. Clearly, something must have changed drastically on the prospect's side. After all, you confirmed the dollar assignment at the end of the first meeting and in a follow-up email. You will need to find out immediately what exactly has changed, potentially determine a new investment amount together with the buyer, and abandon the presentation. Then schedule a new date to present the new solution.

Manage Through Audience Attention Loss

Getting the audience to pay attention throughout the presentation is not easy. The problem is that a typical presentation runs longer than most people can focus on one thing, and with cell phones and even laptops on conference room tables being the new norm, distractions are not far away. During the presentation, the audience's attention naturally wanes.

There are two strategies to avoid this attention loss. You can either make your presentation so short that you have the audience's attention throughout, or you can break the presentation into several shorter sections.

One very effective tactic is to include an interactive element at the end or beginning of each section—for example, a product demonstration, like a spec commercial. Another one is to consistently check in with the audience and ask if they have any questions and like what was presented.

The more personal or professional stories you can weave into the presentation, the better. Audiences pay attention to stories. They make you stand out from other presenters and add an essential ingredient that is not included in the written proposal to your presentation.

"What Do You Think?"

The most important part of the presentation is when you introduce your customized solution to the prospect's challenges. In the previous chapter about written proposals, we listed the corresponding slide to this under the headline "The Concept" (or "The Idea" or "The Strategy"). This is the moment sales champions live for. This is the part they rehearse the most. If there is one thing you should not do now, it's to turn toward the screen. Instead, face your audience and explain the solution with full confidence. Watch the buyers' body language. Are they leaning in? Are they nodding? Smiling? Frowning? Once you are finished, pause to give them a moment to process what they just heard, and then check in with them. This is the moment when sales are made, or lost.

"What do you think?"

"Do you like the idea?"

"Do you think this will help solve the problem?"

Anticipate Concerns

Sales aces proactively weave expected concerns into their presentations, instead of waiting for them to surface at the end of the meeting—or, even worse on a lost deal, never. Done well, it allows you to actually turn something negative into something positive. It also allows you to keep better control of the meeting.

You'll need to apply some discipline when handling questions during a presentation. Yes, you want to encourage the audience as much as possible, to make the proposal meeting more conversational. But you do run the risk of being sidetracked or running out of time if you operate too loosely here. Sometimes buyers will ask a question that you know will be addressed later in the presentation. Tell them you will get to the answer in a bit and move on.

Check In with the Buyer

Taking the buyer's temperature throughout the presentation is essential. Before you move to a different section, check in with them:

"Does that make sense?"

"Did I miss something here?"

"Any questions on this?"

If you notice that something external is distracting your buyer, pause the meeting and ask, *"Do you need to take care of something?"* It would be foolish to just carry on knowing that the decision maker is not paying attention.

There is a moment toward the end of every presentation, when you have covered your entire plan in detail, to stop for a final round of questions. This feels like a good way to close the presentation, doesn't it? It isn't. The old *"That's all I got. Any questions?"* means that you are fully giving up control of the meeting at that point. No matter how often you asked during the presentation, someone will raise their hand and ask something, and as a result you will have no influence over the last topic that is being discussed. Instead, invite your audience for final questions not *after*, but *before* you summarize your solution (the part when you "tell them again"). Go over the key messages and elements one more time, then move on to discuss the best next step.

MASTER THE HOW

When we covered how to make a successful cold call in chapter seven, we discussed that *how* you sound is at least as important as *what* you are saying. A proposal meeting is very similar. You can have the best written proposal, even the best-spoken content—but if your delivery is off, it can cost you the deal.

Mental Preparation

In addition to rehearsing the presentation, you also have to get mentally ready. Olympic sprinters visualize their performances and wins in advance of their races. Once they step on the starting line, they don't look back or sideways—they only look at the finish line. They have done their preparation; now it's time to focus. Sales champions approach proposal meetings in much the same way. They might not go for a gold medal, but at that moment, the presentation is all that counts.

Act and Speak with Confidence

If you are naturally a little more of a low-energy person, you need to find a way to come across as very energetic during the meeting. If you are more of an introvert, this is the time to appear more outgoing than you actually are.

Speak with confidence, smile, make eye contact. A little bit of humor doesn't hurt. The impression you want to give is that you love your job, you love the proposal, and you are excited to be here. You are showing enthusiasm that is contagious, but not in a "salesy" kind of way. Don't underestimate the importance of nonverbal communication, either. If your words, voice, eyes, hands, and body all communicate the same information, your message is reinforced and your audience will receive it.

Final Thoughts on Proposal Presentations

How much time do you allot for your presentation? As a general rule, plan for your presentation to last no longer than half the time allowed. Don't run long, and don't underestimate how long it will take to discuss the questions that might come up at the end of the meeting. You want to leave yourself enough time to cover everything that needs to be covered to move the deal forward.

Personally, I prefer to sit rather than stand when walking buyers through a proposal. It allows for a more conversational approach. Obviously, if it is a larger meeting, with many people from both sides in the room, it can make more sense to stand when presenting.

One last thing to emphasize is the fact that a good proposal meeting is really not as much about the actual written proposal than most people think. There are meetings where you don't need them at all. And sometimes, written proposals can actually hold you back. I have seen more than one sales presentation where the prospect was clearly ready to buy—in fact said so on more than one occasion during the meeting—and the salesperson continued to run through slide after slide, like in the old sales joke, *"Don't buy yet, I'm not finished with my presentation."* When you see an opening to get the deal done, go for it!

ASK

23

WELCOME TO THE KINGDOM OF ASK

B efore I started out in sales, I was fascinated by techniques salespeople used to "close" deals. At the airport, I noticed books titled *Secrets of Closing the Sale* or *The Art of Closing the Sale*. At the bar, I heard friends who worked in sales brag about how they closed a deal. It all made it sound like closing is all there is in sales, and that everything else salespeople are doing is of much less significance.

I couldn't wait—once I got into the business—to finally take a look behind the curtain to learn how salespeople really get deals done, and I was expecting all kinds of hocus-pocus. What I found was . . . not much! I noticed pretty quickly that the most successful salespeople on the team spent much more time preparing for and focusing on the early stages of the sales process, on prospecting, connecting, and discovering. The last thing that was on their minds was trying to somehow trick a dream prospect into doing business with them.

"Closing" seems like a misnomer anyway. It sounds like something is coming to an end, when in reality it is the beginning of the client relationship. "Closing" sounds like something you are doing *to* buyers, when you're actually working *with* them toward a mutual benefit. It also sounds like a onetime act, when it is so much more than that. So let's forget about closing. Instead, let's focus on asking. Not just asking for a final commitment at the end of the sales process, but also asking for mini-commitments throughout the entire sales journey:

- Ask for the decision maker
- Ask for the first meeting
- Ask for permission to follow through with your meeting agenda
- Ask for information during the discovery phase
- Ask for an assignment
- Ask for a budget
- Ask for input to craft a customized solution
- Ask for the proposal meeting
- Ask for the order
- Ask for the signed contract

You get the idea. You might have noticed that in the sales process framework we introduced at the beginning of the book, the Ask phase is shown vertically and aligns with all other steps in the sales process. That's because sales champions ask for mini-commitments at every phase.

ALWAYS BE ASKING

We have all heard the phrase "Always Be Closing." Let's change that to "Always Be Asking." Mini-commitments require buyers to actively agree and follow through. They are the small steps on the long buying journey, and, if done effectively, will get you to your destination, the sale. They are effective because each commitment means buyers are getting more and more invested, emotionally and intellectually. Each commitment makes turning back harder for them.

If you received many "yeses" throughout the sales process, asking for the order can actually feel like an anticlimactic formality, the natural outcome of taking buyers through your process. And it certainly doesn't require a special technique or an entire rehearsed script. Of course, if you miss getting all these prior commitments, asking for the final commitment will be by far the most challenging step in the sales process. You cannot move the final Ask forward by skipping the Asks that should have come before.

IT'S YOU WHO MUST ASK FOR THE ORDER

It's your job to keep the ball rolling and your job to ask for the order, directly and assertively. Your buyer will not do it for you. When you fail to ask for the order, you will fail. If you have done everything appropriately during the sales process up until this moment, you have earned the right to ask for this final commitment. Buyers know that you are a salesperson and that you are meeting with them to eventually sell them something. It's not a secret. There is no reason to be uncomfortable asking for the commitments you need to help your prospect solve their challenges. If you have built enough trust in the process, this conversation should feel really natural.

KEEP YOUR EMOTIONAL DISCIPLINE

The final Ask can certainly be a little bit more nerve-racking than all the other Asks. After all, you have invested a lot of time and energy into the deal, and the last thing you want is for it to fall through in the final second. You might have even mentally allocated your commission dollars and maybe could win this month's sales contest if your buyer agrees to proceed. But if there is a time to keep your emotional discipline, this is it.

Try to anticipate the anxiety that comes right before asking for the order. Visualize how the buyer agrees to your proposal and practice self-talk to manage your emotions. The good news is that the more deals you get done, the more you hear *"I'm in"* from a buyer, the easier it will be to ask for the order the next time around. That's the reason why salespeople typically close more, better deals at fewer discounts when they've already exceeded their quota for the quarter. Their confidence is higher and their perceived risk lower. If, on the other hand, their pipeline is empty and they desperately need a close to get anywhere near their quota, their anxiety will be higher.

ASSUME YOUR DEAL WILL CLOSE

When asking for the order, *how* you sound is at least as important as *what* you say. You have to come across as confident, strong, and in control of the process. Many sales pros do that by taking an assumptive position that then translates into the words they are actually saying:

"Here is what we are going to do."

They are assuming the deal will proceed and acting accordingly.

SOUND NATURAL, NOT SCRIPTED

You don't want to sound overly rehearsed, and that's why working off scripts during this stage of the sales process is not advisable, despite all the closing tips you can find in sales books. You need to have a very fluid back-and-forth conversation with the buyer, and following a prewritten script is more hindrance than help.

Instead, the best salespeople weave the Ask for the order very naturally into the conversation:

- *"This will work for you. Let's do it."*
- *"I think we have a good plan in place. All we need to get started is your approval and a signed agreement."*
- *"So why don't we go ahead and get this started."*
- *"If this works for you, let's go ahead and get the contract drafted."*
- *"Okay, let's lock this in now."*

ASK FOR LONG-TERM COMMITMENTS

And while you are at it, try to push for a long-term commitment. What's the worst thing that can happen? The buyer won't agree to it, and you'll have to revert to a shorter contract length than planned. That's not ideal, of course, but it is also not the end of the world. Pushing for a longer-term commitment doesn't usually jeopardize the deal. "If you ask, you get; if you don't, you won't," a colleague of mine used to say.

The fact is, many buyers will absolutely consider a longer-term commitment, especially if they come with an additional incentive. In many situations, long term is also better for the prospect. People like stability and hate change. It certainly is much better for you, on many levels. A long-term contract completely changes the dynamic with a buyer. You are no longer a vendor who comes to beg for renewals every few months. Instead, you are a true resource to the client, a strategic partner that becomes an extension of their business. Long-term commitments are how lifelong client relationships are made. The fact that they also keep your competitors at bay is a nice side effect.

SAY NOTHING

Once you ask for the order, take a deep breath. Then, do and say nothing. Just wait and see what happens and watch the buyer closely. Doing nothing, of course, sounds very easy. It is not. After all, this is the most exciting part of your entire sales journey so far with the buyer. You will be tempted to elaborate, to overexplain and potentially talk past the Ask. Give the buyer space to think and to answer. And trust me, answer they will.

THE BUYER SAYS YES

They might answer in the affirmative. Congratulations! Your bag of "yeses," as a result of your asking for micro-commitments throughout the sales process, was full enough to lead to this result. Don't lose your composure now. Shake the buyer's hand and tell them how much you are looking forward to working together on the implementation of the program. Then define the next steps. Depending on the industry you are in and the size of the sale you made, these can be different things:

- A signed agreement that you brought to the proposal meeting
- A contract that still needs to be drafted by your legal department and negotiated with the buyer and his legal team
- A follow-up meeting with a third party that needs to be involved in the final evaluation and potentially final negotiation of the deal, like the purchasing department or a media agency
- A payment in the form of a credit card payment, check, wire transfer, or digital payment
- Especially in more complex negotiations, the follow-up document might be a Letter of Intent or a Letter of Understanding that captures what was agreed upon and states what still needs to be negotiated

After you agree on the next step with the buyer, leave. There's no reason to hang around. Your business is done for the time being and the last thing you want is for the buyer to change his mind, even if only on some minor details. Say *"Thank you"* and tell the buyer you will start executing the next step right away.

THE BUYER HAS CONCERNS

What if buyers don't say *"yes,"* though? What if they aren't ready to move forward with your proposal? As we have discussed, you need to actively draw out issues and questions the buyer might have throughout the presentation of your proposal. I am deliberately using the term "concern" and not "objection" here, because if you have embarked on the sales journey with a buyer together, gone through all the motions and Asks, followed your process, and involved the buyer in it, no buyer will—suddenly and out of nowhere—raise his hand and scream *"Objection!"* like a trial lawyer does in court. This absolutely happens at an earlier stage of the sales process, when you are trying to connect with a buyer you don't know yet. But it shouldn't happen now. Buyers certainly can voice concerns about proceeding to the next step with a deal, though, and you will need to address them and bring the conversation to a mutually beneficial conclusion.

First of all, stay calm. Dealing with concerns is part of your job. It's normal and shouldn't come as a surprise. That means you can prepare for it. What makes concerns a little different from the objections and dismissals we encountered during the Connect phase of the sales process is that, while there is a pretty finite list of potential objections and dismissals you need to anticipate when making a cold call, the potential list of concerns a buyer can have at this final stage of the sales process can be much longer:

"We love the idea, but won't have money for it until next year."

"I don't think I am getting enough value."

"I like it, but I need to take it to the board."

"Your company was just in the news for lack of diversity."

"We're going to stick with what we have been using."

"I am just not sure I will be getting the results I need to get to show positive ROI."

"My colleague saw some negative reviews of your product online."

There are many, many more potential concerns. That means you can't have a script or line ready at your fingertips for each one of them.

DEALING WITH CONCERNS

Most salespeople will push back instantly when their buyers voice concerns over the solution, trying to change their mind right then and there. As a result, what was a cordial business conversation can quickly turn acrimonious. You can't just shoot down a concern and expect the buyer to simply agree with your side of the argument. Others abandon their entire solution—that they spent many hours brainstorming and building out—way too quickly, only because of one minor concern by the buyer and because they want to avoid friction.

Instead, your best strategy is to gather more information from the buyer.

In chapter twelve we introduced a framework on how to deal with real objections thrown at you while initially approaching prospects. This framework also works great for dealing with concerns at the end of the sales process, just with minor modifications, since you now have much more information about the companies' challenges and goals than you had during your cold call. Again, you first **sympathize** and **acknowledge** that you heard the buyer's concern. This gives you a moment to gather your thoughts and to control your emotions. Then, ask for overall buy-in to the proposal and concept you presented. This is necessary to establish that there isn't a much bigger issue with your proposal. Maybe you misunderstood something earlier in the sales process; maybe things have drastically changed on the prospect's end that simply don't make your proposal feasible. You need to establish that before you move on.

> Buyer: *"I really need to think about this a little more before I commit. It's a big commitment."*
>
> You: *"I get your concern. With a decision like this it makes sense to think it through from all angles. Does the concept make sense to you, though? Do you like the idea?"*

If your proposal is way off base, don't keep pushing for an order right now. Instead, offer to go back to the drawing board and schedule a follow-up meeting with them. If buyers tell you they like what you presented and are proposing, follow up with a couple of **open-ended questions** to clarify you understood the concern correctly and uncover more information about why the buyers have it. You need to know in as much detail as possible why the buyer's decision is currently set to "no." Sometimes buyers are not always clear when they voice concerns, and some buyers can even be a bit dishonest about them. It is your job to cut through the smoke and mirrors. You also want to determine if the concern is the only one the buyer has at this moment, or if there are others:

> *"What's your main concern with what I showed you? What part of it don't you like?"*

Based on what the buyer is telling you, your next move is to **position** your proposal in a way that addresses your buyer's concern. The best way to do that is by reminding buyers of the challenges they shared with you during the first meeting, and how your proposal helps solve them. You are a businessperson, here to help. You need to diplomatically bring across the point that if they keep their money (instead of giving it to you in exchange for your solution), they will also keep their problem. In our example, that means reminding them of what their current status quo is costing them, or making them miss out on. If you did a thorough discovery job in the first meeting, you will even be able to back this up with numbers. Your ultimate goal here is to maximize the benefit your proposal is delivering to the prospect, while minimizing the importance of their voiced concern.

Then **ask for the order** again, assumptively and confidently.

> *"Based on that, it doesn't seem to make sense to me to wait with the implementation. Every day you are losing is costing you. So why don't we go ahead and get our legal teams to draft the contract?"*

Is this easy to do? No, sales is not easy, even if your friends think so.

THE BUYER SAYS NO

Despite your best efforts, more often than not you won't be able to alleviate the buyer's concerns, and your deal will not move forward. Many factors play into their decisions, and not all of them are in your control. Understand that the cards are stacked against you, simply because the status quo is usually much more convenient for the buyer. It carries no potential disruption while shifting from one partner to another. There is no personal risk in being the one having championed the change internally. There will be no uncomfortable conversation with the current vendor, potentially a long-term partner of the company and maybe even a friend of the buyer. The status quo is king. And kings are not easily toppled.

If you do receive a clear *"no,"* make sure you at least get to an agreement with the buyer that what was turned down was not you and not the company you are working for, but your proposal, and your proposal alone. That keeps the door open for future opportunities. Thinking in Salesforce terms, you are only closing out an opportunity—not the lead.

Once you are back at your office, debrief with your team. What are the lessons? Where did we fall short? What could we have done differently? What's the next step with this prospect?

YOUR DEAL IS STUCK

You will run into situations where buyers seem interested, but, despite your best attempts, won't give you the go-ahead. In other words, your deal is stuck.

Sales champions prepare for this going into the proposal meeting and don't just shoot from the hip when a delayed decision causes trouble. Among the strategies they will consider are:

- Carving up the proposal into manageable chunks. Big concepts with big budgets are riskier for buyers and harder to get through the system. Start smaller, with a smaller challenge and goal. Demonstrate that you are delivering results, then work your way up from there. We all would love to do the monster deal off the bat, but sometimes it's just not possible. Mark Hunter writes in *High-Profit Prospecting*, "Never forgo the first sale for the sake of landing the big sale." At least you have your foot in the door and can build a personal relationship with the decision maker. It will be logical for your buyer to give you more business if you do a good job.

- Offering to start working on deliverables, even if you don't have a final agreement yet. *"What does your timeline look like? Let's use the time between now and then to work on creative, should you decide to go forward."*
- Creating urgency by leveraging demand on inventory and setting deadlines and rate expiration dates.
- Having a senior executive of your company reach out and offer to meet and become an executive sponsor for implementing the solution.
- If the buyer is telling you that your proposal needs to be reviewed and approved by additional people within their company, offer to be there. *"As you go over this with your team, there is no doubt they will have questions and maybe even concerns. I want to make sure that I am here to address all the questions that come up. When is the meeting?"*

Sometimes, you will have to be patient and let things run their course. During this time, don't become another salesperson pestering the buyer by *"just checking in."* Instead, while you await a decision on your proposal, provide value. Show them that you keep doing your homework and have another insight about their consumer or their competitors. Tell them that you have been thinking about their business and potential opportunities. In short, at least have some kind of relevant business reason for your follow-up. That's how you set yourself apart from the rest of the salespeople, who are *"just calling to find out where we stand with our proposal."*

"ARE YOU OKAY?"

Even the best salespeople get "ghosted" by buyers, with all of their attempts to get in touch with them in vain. Eventually, you will have to change your tactics. What I have seen working is—after a while—to send an email with the core message of *"Are you okay?"* Frame it as a very personal note, even implying that you were concerned for their health. A very similar tactic is to state in your email that you thought they were interested, but perhaps you misjudged the situation, since you haven't gotten a response to any of your prior emails. Many balls that were stuck have started rolling again after messages like these, simply because buyers might have felt guilty about their lack of responsiveness. Even if they respond and tell you they are no longer considering your proposal, it is beneficial to you. At least you know where you stand and (if the prospect is worth pursuing further) can plan the next step.

CASE STUDY:
ASKING REBECCA GYMS FOR THE ORDER
AND DEALING WITH THEIR CONCERNS

You: *"If this works for you, let's go ahead and get the contract drafted."*

Tracy: *"Not yet. I want to shop around a little bit more, so I can't give you my final decision right now."*

You: *"Got it. Never a bad idea to see what the marketplace has to offer. Does our campaign make sense to you, though? Do you like the idea of creating a Rebecca Gyms movement together with our female on-air personalities?"*

Tracy: *"I like it a lot, actually. It's well thought out."*

You: *"So you really don't have any concerns about the proposal itself, it's really more about getting more market intel?"*

Tracy: *"Exactly."*

You: *"I am just curious. What in particular are you trying to accomplish by opening this up to more companies?"*

Tracy: *"It's really mostly due diligence. I want to make sure I will be getting the most bang for my buck."*

You: *"I promise I will work with you on the value we are delivering. You and I spoke about delivering a minimum of 1,500 trial memberships by December 31. And you said that would be a massive success in that short period of time in a new market, correct?"*

Tracy: *"Yes, it definitely would be."*

You: *"Our campaign will deliver that for you. Tracy, you are only a few months away from your launch and we still need to draft the contract, finalize the agreements with your spokespeople, come up with the right creative for the campaign, and, of course, reserve the on-air and digital inventory, which as you know is in high demand for Christmas. And you told me the next few months will be the busiest you and your team will ever be."*

Tracy: *"Q4 will be a crazy time. I don't even want to think about it."*

You: *"Then let me help you by being the extended marketing arm that you will need. I can handle a lot of this. It seems to me that getting started with the execution of our campaign is better time spent than chasing a couple more salespeople for proposals that you most likely won't need and use."*

Tracy: *"You are right. I hadn't looked at it that way. But you have to work with me on the price."*

You: *"I will. In the meantime, why don't we go ahead and get our legal teams to start working on the contract."*

24

WINNING IN SALES NEGOTIATIONS

I hadn't planned to write this chapter, primarily because it is almost impossible to teach good negotiation tactics over the course of a few pages. There are certainly enough books about it, and if you want to start with one, may I suggest the old classic *You Can Negotiate Anything* by Herb Cohen. When it comes to sales negotiation, there are also significant differences between industries, and one-size solutions and tips that work in all situations are few and far between. The reason I ended up including it are two sales calls that I participated in when I was nearly done writing this book. On both occasions, salespeople literally left several hundred thousand dollars on the table while concluding a new business deal. While I won't get into too much detail here, I want to highlight several effective negotiation tactics that I have seen work for successful salespeople.

NEGOTIATION MISTAKES CAN COST YOU DEARLY

Most salespeople are the worst negotiators in the world. Really, that's true. As soon as a buyer puts pressure on them, they crumble. Most want deals to happen so badly that they are willing to sacrifice the company's margins and their own income. Just do the math. If you propose a $20,000 a month program to a new client, but end up agreeing to $17,000, and this client continues to do business with you at this investment level for three years, you cost your company $108,000. At a 10 percent commission rate, you left $10,800 in commission on the table. That's already a lot of money, but just picture how this could hurt you financially over the course of your career, with many more clients and deals and discounts that are potentially much larger than our example.

MOST PEOPLE DON'T ENJOY NEGOTIATING

The best-case scenario for salespeople, of course, is no negotiation. The buyer liked the proposal enough to give you the okay at the price point you had originally included in the proposal. If you were proactive throughout the sales process, proved your value, and had an open conversation about budgets and dollars even before you presented your solution, this is absolutely an achievable outcome, even more so because in the Western world most people don't feel comfortable negotiating and actually try to avoid it. Travel to the Balkans or Southeast Asia and you will find negotiating is the modus operandi on anything they sell.

We have already mentioned that being assertive and assumptive is a good frame of mind in many sales aspects, and it is no different during sales negotiations. Approach the buyer with the confident assumption that the buyer will agree to your proposal without negotiating.

BUYERS HAVE THE INITIAL ADVANTAGE

In many sales situations, buyers will be in a better negotiating position than you from the start. Why? Simply because they will most likely consider alternatives besides you. It is in their best interest to do so, and many will take advantage of it and play different salespeople against each other. It's your job to use your sales skills and everything we covered throughout this book to eliminate as many of these alternatives as possible. A full pipeline on your side is your way to level the negotiation playing field, at least mentally. If you have several other big deals about to happen or already struck, you will approach the next negotiation with much more confidence.

EFFECTIVE NEGOTIATING STRATEGIES

To quote Jeb Blount in *Inked*, an excellent book about sales negotiation: "Effective negotiators are masters at aligning the sales process, buying process, and decision process."

They do this by using several different negotiating strategies effectively.

Proposal First, Negotiation Second

Great sales negotiators try to separate the solution they are proposing to the buyer from the negotiation as much as possible. In other words, they try to get buy-in for their proposal first, and only then are they willing to focus on price. That makes a lot of sense, because if you have not yet been implicitly or explicitly selected as the future partner, you are in essence negotiating with yourself. Way too often, salespeople give away things way too early in the process.

Statements like, *"I'll put together a proposal, and by the way, the timing is great, we are currently giving new clients a 20 percent discount on the first order"* during the first meeting or, *"We also have a lower-priced option"* in the proposal meeting will do nothing but cost you money and commission. In the first example, you already lowered the price by 20 percent before the negotiation even started. In the second example, you will most likely walk away with the lower-priced option (in the end, most likely sold at an even lower price than the lower price you had in mind!).

But how do you know if you have "won" so that you can start your negotiation? Sometimes, buyers will tell you outright, like Tracy Ranner did in the Rebecca Gyms case study in the previous chapter, or with statements like *"I want to work with you, but . . ."* Sometimes, you will have to search for clues or—especially on larger deals—find ways to get more information from internal coaches about the status of your proposal.

Offer More Value

Rather than lowering your pricing, offer more value for the same financial investment. Before you start negotiating, come up with a list of items that have relatively low value to you and don't cost you much (or nothing at all), but are important to and have high value for the buyer. Offer to add them to the existing proposal. These items can be related to the proposal (in the media industry, for example, additional no-charge impressions in dayparts that a TV or radio station has unsold inventory available to use) or not (an exclusive money-can't-buy experience to which you have access).

Propose Creative Payment Solutions

There are many examples of how thinking out of the box on payment led to a positive outcome for both prospect and seller. Can you shift things into a new fiscal year, extend more flexible payment terms, or charge less up front? Whatever it is, work closely with your finance department on it to avoid overpromising and then discovering that what you suggested is not doable, or even illegal.

Give and Take

Sometimes, you will have to lower the investment level you initially included in your proposal. Instead of heedlessly starting to give discounts, determine which elements of your proposal could be excluded in return for a lower price. Ideally, these items will be of high value to you, and of low value to buyers. They are losing something they don't consider that important and paying less. What's not to like?

Negotiate Lower in Small Increments

If you have to show some flexibility on price and have exhausted other options, do it in irregular increments. Average salespeople often make the mistake to "try to meet in the middle." Your initial Ask was $250,000, your buyer offered $200,000, so you split the difference and agree to $225,000. That's not a good idea! You want to start with a smaller increment that ideally is not a round number, maybe something like $245,750, and if the buyer again counters, come back with a smaller concession, to signal to the buyer that your willingness to negotiate on price is coming to an end—for example, $244,500.

Be Quiet

From the previous chapter you will remember our tactic of remaining silent after asking for the order. The same applies to a sales negotiation. Uncomfortable silences can actually work to your advantage. Make your counteroffer and then be quiet. Sometimes buyers will try to break what seems like an impasse to them by making another offer.

Play the Higher-Authority Game

The vast majority of the time during my sales career, I left my manager at the office and negotiated with buyers on my own. I wanted to have the flexibility to tell buyers that I don't have the authority to agree to certain concessions they were demanding. Instead of being forced to react on the spot to things that I felt needed a little more thought and consideration, I worked out all other outstanding items in the negotiation, then got back to them on the final concession at a later point. Use this higher-authority strategy to your advantage. When almost the entire contract has been negotiated, rarely will a buyer walk away because of one last item.

I sometimes hear from sellers who are unhappy about the fact that their sales manager doesn't give them full negotiation authority. Don't be.

It can work to your advantage. But, of course, make sure you are getting clear instructions from your manager on what your negotiation limits are.

Take the Deal Off the Table

It is not uncommon that the first counteroffer from the buyer is completely unreasonable and you will need to determine if it even makes sense to continue the negotiation. What can be effective in a situation like this is to take the proposal off the table. Here are two examples:

"I'd really love to work with you, but it seems we are just way too far apart with this particular proposal. It will make more sense to come up with a completely different and smaller solution."

"If I can't do that, how can we still work together?"

If you did a good job throughout the sales process and your initial proposal was strong enough to solve the prospect's challenges, most likely buyers will insist on the original solution you presented. And with that, your negotiating position will have improved dramatically.

Don't Get Emotional

Your ability to stay objective throughout the negotiation will be crucial to a positive outcome. If you are emotionally attached to any single issue or—much worse—lose your cool or even your temper, you will compromise your ability to negotiate. Don't fight to win a battle, then lose the war. Buyers will hopefully soon be your clients, and you will have to work with them. However hard you negotiate, always protect the relationship with buyers.

Negotiate with the Right Person

There is nothing more frustrating than finding out at the end of a negotiation that the person you negotiated with didn't have full authority to make a deal. Don't ever put yourself in this position. That's why determining early in the sales process how decisions are being made and signed off on is crucial.

CASE STUDY: FINALIZING THE DEAL WITH REBECCA GYMS

In the previous chapter, you came to a preliminary agreement with Tracy Ranner, CMO of Rebecca Gyms, on partnering for Rebecca Gyms' launch campaign.

> **Tracy:** *"You are right. I hadn't looked at it that way. But you have to work with me on the price."*
>
> **You:** *"I will. In the meantime, why don't we go ahead and get our legal teams to start working on the contract."*

Now, let's try to come to a mutually beneficial agreement on price and value:

> **Tracy:** *"When I look at the media value and impressions you included in the proposal, I just don't think we are getting enough for our money."*
>
> **You:** *"I get why it can seem that way. Right now the campaign delivers just short of 95 million media impressions, though, and even in a market like New York that is a massive amount of impressions. It will generate reach and frequency, and with that, brand awareness, very quickly."*
>
> **Tracy:** *"I don't disagree with that, but your cost per thousand impressions is much higher than what we are paying our partners in Los Angeles."*

You: *"Yes, and there is a reason for it. Impression comparisons are not always apples-to-apples comparisons. Just think about it: a quick five-second billboard on the radio delivers a certain amount of impressions, and so does a thirty-second live endorsement by one of your spokespeople. These live endorsement impressions are much more impactful than the short :5s, but both count as the same number of impressions. Our program is almost exclusively built around our longer influencer announcements, and that's why the CPM is higher. Make sense?"*

Tracy: *"Yes. But I still need you to be lower. I really don't think I can do the $794,500 you proposed. Can you do the program for $725,000? Don't forget, it's the first time we are working together. There will be more business down the line for you."*

You: *"I would have to take certain elements out of the campaign, for example some of the on-site appearances of our on-air talent that are included in the proposal. But I do get your concern about giving this a little bit more meat. What if we add five million media impressions to the campaign? We would just need flexibility how and when we would run them. But yes, I can guarantee your message would be heard five million more times."*

Tracy: *"That's much better. And we will need every single one of them. What can you do price-wise, though? When I told you we want to work with you, you promised to work with me on it."*

You: *"I really can't go much lower, Tracy. This is a really comprehensive campaign, and with the additional five million impressions, also really efficient."*

Tracy: *"Let's say $750,000 and we have a deal."*

You: *"I wish I could. If I lower your evening rates, I can bring the overall investment down to $787,500."*

Tracy: *"$775,000."*

You: *"$785,000, and I'll get my wife to sign up for a trial membership."*

Tracy: *"Deal! Can't wait to get started working on the execution."*

LAUNCH

THIS IS JUST THE START

C ongratulations, you have earned the sale. You won. You are a sales champion. Now what?

American economist and Harvard professor Theodore Levitt said, "When the salesperson finally makes the sale, the salesperson's anxiety ends and the customer's anxiety begins." Rarely have words described this immediate post-sale phase better. However, Mr. Levitt should have used the term "average salesperson." That's because sales aces use this situation to their advantage and stand out from the competition by making their new client feel confident they made the right decision. They think of the first sale not as the "end" of the process, but the beginning of a long-term relationship with a client who can be a great source of profitable repeat business and referrals. How they do it is what we will be discussing in this last chapter of the book.

EXECUTION RESPONSIBILITIES

Some companies structure their sales organization so that salespeople hand over client relationships to account managers, whose responsibility it is to manage the execution of the solution and the future client relationship. At other companies, the salesperson is in charge of 100 percent of the work that comes with the implementation of the solution. The spectrum runs wide. Most likely, you will find yourself somewhere in between, working closely with buyers and their teams as well as your own internal teams on the implementation of sold programs.

SELL INTERNALLY

If you want to succeed in sales, you will have to learn how to sell within your own company as much as to new prospects. You will need to gain commitments from internal stakeholders and ensure they do the work necessary to bring your program to life. These colleagues probably will not work in sales, but in sales operations, marketing, or other back-office departments, like traffic and continuity departments in the broadcasting industry (the department that generates and plans commercial logs). You will need to find a way to get all of them on your side and make them your allies.

I once worked with a salesperson who was great at generating new business, but could be a little bit arrogant and selfish at the office. His orders were always the most important ones and, of course, always came last minute. As a result, the traffic and continuity manager was not necessarily one of his biggest fans. And as a result, his client's commercials ended up being scheduled four to five commercials into the commercial break instead of at the beginning, and in dayparts with less audience. Obviously, that's not very conducive to a successful campaign, and indeed, it didn't end well. Don't underestimate how important it is to build internal alliances. You will need to get your colleagues to do their best work for you.

GET MANAGEMENT ON BOARD

Sales champions also lobby internally with management to ensure that all potential internal obstacles are removed. They get management up to speed not just on the dollar amount they just secured for the company, but also on the results the new client is expecting to see from the sold solution. And they paint a positive picture about the future possibilities and growth opportunities with this client. Ideally, they find an executive sponsor, a huge advantage when it comes to pushing through projects internally, especially when an implementation doesn't go according to plan.

ACCURATE ORDER INPUT IS CRITICAL

I am always stunned by how many mistakes happen during the internal order input. You did all this work, for weeks or even months, came up with all these great concepts, got the client to agree to work with you. And then, you, or someone you work with, doesn't pay enough attention when entering the order. Wrong product quantities, wrong delivery dates, wrong specifications, wrong whatever. Don't confirm Levitt's quote now. Be as accurate as possible and check order confirmations religiously. Many commission dollars have been lost by sloppiness at this stage of the execution.

PROJECT EXECUTION PLAN

Depending on the size of the sold solution, it might be necessary to schedule a meeting with all internal stakeholders to gain commitments from everyone on their deliverables. The result of this meeting is a detailed Project Execution Plan that includes what needs to be done by whom and by when, and is usually created as a shared document that everyone working on the project can access and update in real time. These plans should include any tasks that clients and their teams must perform, again with clearly established timelines and responsibilities. Often, project executions run into problems not because your internal team doesn't deliver, but because someone on your client's team—although usually not the buyers themselves—dropped the ball.

SUPPORT BUYERS WITH THEIR INTERNAL ROLL-OUT

Schedule a follow-up meeting with your new client to determine how the project should be rolled out to the client's team. Who needs to know about it? Who still needs to be convinced? Who needs to be involved in the implementation? Be an asset for the client with this. Offer to host meetings at the client's location or maybe even at a restaurant to bring everyone up to speed. Schedule regular execution meetings that can turn into status meetings after your program launches.

MANAGING EXPECTATIONS

Sales champions make sure that there are no surprises throughout the implementation process. They share the Project Execution Plan and walk the client through all steps:

"This is when you will receive our suggestions on creative."

"This is when we are planning to send out the press release."

"This is what the invoice will look like."

"This is how often you will get updates on the results we are seeing on our end."

Discuss the clients' expectations on how often they would like to get together and receive updates from you, then try to beat their expectations. What materials do they need from you for presentations to their manager or even the board? Who else should you meet at the company to ensure everything runs smoothly, from Accounts Payable to the person in charge of the call center? Every client situation is unique and it is your job to adapt accordingly.

CAMPAIGN LAUNCH NEWSLETTER

Nothing is more critical than to get off to a great start when the implementation is completed and a campaign or solution is ready to be launched or delivered. I have seen sales aces follow this wisdom by composing "Campaign Launch Newsletters" they send to clients on launch day. They include a quick summary and reminder of the program and its goals, and highlight execution elements clients can share with their teams. They also use these newsletters to thank everyone at the client who was involved in the implementation. This is a great idea! Not many salespeople are doing this, and newsletters like these will make you stand out. In addition, have your executive sponsor reach out to senior executives at the client on launch day to congratulate them and thank them for the partnership.

SELL EARLY RESULTS IMMEDIATELY

We covered in chapter thirteen how quickly people tend to make up their mind when meeting new people. They evaluate new solutions, new campaigns, and new projects very quickly, too. Sending clients early positive signs and feedback as well as strong initial results can immediately remind your client of your solution's worth. The best salespeople don't just count on the client to find out about strong initial results on their own. They actively resell clients on them the moment the campaign launches. And that means recapping early and often. Don't let clients wait for weeks until they receive status updates. If you do, and results fall short of your agreed-upon goals, it will be too late to influence their opinions or adjust your solution.

Once your solution is "live," stay fully focused on delivering results. There was a reason that you and the client defined what success looks like and what type of return on investment they expect. Don't avoid this conversation now. If results are not as strong as your client expected, you need to address it. Trying to bury the data and hoping your client won't notice is a surefire way of running into trouble later and not getting a renewal. Many projects and programs have several objectives. While achieving all of them at the same time can be tough, make sure you highlight and sell the ones that are being met. Then work on optimizing your solution in partnership with the client to catch up on the remaining ones.

EXEMPLARY SERVICE AND EXECUTION LEAD TO RENEWALS

Effective execution is the key to a renewal and future growth with the client. It is also the key to getting connected to other decision makers at the client's company. Try to improve your depth of contact with the goal of receiving additional assignments for different lines of business, projects, and brands. Exemplary service throughout the implementation and after the launch also protects you from competitors trying to steal the business. In addition, successful execution ultimately will allow you to create case studies you can use when talking to other new business prospects.

The more and closer you work with clients, the better results you deliver for them, the more they will trust you. And in sales, trust is everything. You can offer the best product or service, but without trust, relationships collapse and future deals are almost impossible to make. By consistently educating your clients, and by identifying and solving their problems, they will come to perceive you as a true resource. That's how you started the relationship at the beginning of the sales process—by offering insights and case studies as well as sharing ideas—and that's how you will win follow-up assignments and grow the business in the future.

At that point, though, we are no longer talking about effective new business generation, but effective account management and upsell strategies. And that's a story that will have to be told in another book.

ACKNOWLEDGMENTS

March 16, 2020, was the first day I ever worked from home. The coronavirus was about to devastate the entire world, and my beloved New York City would be hit especially hard. That first day working out of a quickly assembled home office was the day I committed myself to emerge from this strange period with something I could eventually look back on, maybe even with a little bit of pride. Getting a dog was not possible because of our two cats, Rocky and Elvis, so I decided on the next best thing: writing a book.

It wasn't easy, that I have to admit. Especially at the beginning, I struggled to find a rhythm, and with a day job that easily takes up ten to twelve hours of time every weekday, the only time left for writing was evenings and weekends. A little more than 450 hours later, and with the country reopening, the end result is in your hands. Thank you for picking up the book. That alone shows you are on the way to becoming a sales champion. I am humbled that you looked to me for advice, and hope you will find the material useful in your day-to-day business. I would love to hear your feedback at aceit.bernieweiss@gmail.com.

Thank you to iHeartMedia chief executive officer Bob Pittman for contributing the foreword to this book. Bob is one of the few people who actually are "Natural Born Salespeople." He is so charismatic and knowledgeable that he can get deals done even if he skips several steps in the sales process. Don't model your sales approach after Bob!

A big thank-you to the entire iHeartMedia Multiplatform Group leadership, who have created a culture that encourages the sharing of best sales practices across all of the 150 iHeartMedia markets. Thank you to

CEO Greg Ashlock, President Hartley Adkins, and Division President Scott Hopeck.

This book would have not been possible without all the knowledge gained from the best sales force in the world, the iHeartMedia New York sales team. Over the years, I certainly learned more from them than they learned from me. And this doesn't just include the account executives with long track records—like Jamie Meintanas, Jill Oliva, Scott Berliner, Jason Roy and Matt Parisi—who have mastered many of the new sales tools and technologies available, but also the younger sellers and managers. Carolyn Whitman, Jessie Lessin, Katerina Karousos, and Ben Henry, all of whom provided many useful tips on social selling that made it into the book, deserve a special mention here. Nicole Wendel turned my handwritten charts into professional illustrations.

Over the course of writing this book, I also spoke with many clients and asked them for input. After all, they are on the receiving end of cold calls, emails, and presentations. Their input was invaluable. Thank you!

Over the years, several people planted the seed in my mind of eventually writing a book. One of them was Guenther Richter, father of my old friend, Clemens Richter, whose heartfelt short stories about Krems, my hometown in Austria, were published just a few years ago—when he was already in his seventies. One of them includes a reference to me, so I am returning the favor here!

Longtime publishing executive Larry Olsen was instrumental in making this book happen. His introduction to Matt Holt at Matt Holt Books and BenBella is proof of the power of referrals covered in the book. Thank you, Matt and BenBella Books, and the entire team working on the book: Leah Wilson, Sarah Avinger, Alyn Wallace, Adrienne Lang, Alicia Kania, Susan Welte, Sarah Beck, Jay Kilburn, Mallory Hyde, and James Fraleigh, the best copyeditor in the business (and a fellow Depeche Mode fan).

Dean Karrel took the time to explain the nuts and bolts of the publishing industry to me and introduced me to Debra Englander, whose initial editorial guidance was invaluable. Cal Hunter at Barnes & Noble allowed me a look behind the curtain of retail book sales and made sure I knew the ins and outs of in-store promotions. Thank you!

There are no words to convey my gratitude to my mother, Helga Weiss, who raised four children—Eva, Georg, Stefan, and me—on her own, making an infinite number of personal sacrifices along the way. Her character example has shaped me more than anything else. So has a German quote that my late father, Helmut Weiss, shared with me when I was seven years old. It has always stuck with me and actually hangs on the wall of my New York office: "Das Salz des Schweisses hat mehr heilende Kraft als das Salz der Traenen": the salt of sweat has more healing power than the salt of tears. Since my father's death in 1992, it has become my mantra.

Lastly, but most important, the love of my life, my wife, Khartoon Weiss. Her insight, wisdom, and energy guided me through all chapters of this book. She is the most remarkable person I know.

INDEX

ABOUT THE AUTHOR

BERNIE WEISS is president of iHeartMedia New York. After starting out selling radio advertising for a New York-based hip-hop station, he rose quickly through the sales and sales management ranks of iHeart-Media, America's #1 audio company, and is now overseeing some of the most prestigious radio station brands in the world. Over the course of twenty years, Bernie has coached hundreds of salespeople—rookies and veterans—many of whom went on to become sales superstars and rose to leadership positions themselves. He lives in New York City.